Clairvoyance
For Beginners

About the Author

Alexandra Chauran is a second-generation fortune-teller, a third-degree elder High Priestess of British Traditional Wicca, and the Queen of a coven. As a professional psychic intuitive for more than a decade, she serves thousands of clients in the Seattle area and globally through her website. She is certified in tarot and has been interviewed on National Public Radio and other major media outlets. Alexandra is currently pursuing a doctoral degree, lives in Issaquah, Washington, and can be found online at EarthShod.com.

Clairvoyance

For Beginners

Easy Techniques to
Enhance Your Psychic Visions

ALEXANDRA CHAURAN

Llewellyn Publications
Woodbury, Minnesota

FIRST EDITION
First Printing, 2014

Book format by Bob Gaul
Cover art: Shutterstock.com/35287888/©Lia Koltyrina
           Digital Stock Corporation/088/©NASA
Cover design by Ellen Lawson
Editing by Laura Graves

Llewellyn Publications is a registered trademark of Llewellyn Worldwide Ltd.

Library of Congress Cataloging-in-Publication Data
Chauran, Alexandra, 1981–
  Clairvoyance for beginners: easy techniques to enhance your psychic
visions/Alexandra Chauran.—First Edition.
      pages cm
  Includes bibliographical references.
  ISBN 978-0-7387-3915-1
1. Clairvoyance. I. Title.
  BF1325.C465 2014
  133.8'4—dc23
                          2014006543

Llewellyn Publications
A Division of Llewellyn Worldwide Ltd.
2143 Wooddale Drive
Woodbury, MN 55125-2989
www.llewellyn.com

Printed in the United States of America

Other books by Alexandra Chauran

Crystal Ball Reading for Beginners
Faeries & Elementals for Beginners
Have You Been Hexed?
Palmistry Every Day
So You Want to Be a Psychic Intuitive?

*This book is dedicated to my "clear seeing"
acquisitions editor, Amy Glaser; production editor
Laura Graves; all the revision and proofreading
editors at Llewellyn Worldwide who work on my
books as a team; and my mother, who has carefully
gone over each of my books and set me straight if I've
muddled things up! Thank you all for your vision.*

contents

introduction

When I was in college, everyone in my dorm knew I was a clairvoyant. You see, the walls were paper thin, and I was working for one of those psychic hotlines in which I would give clairvoyant readings over the phone. My next-door neighbor in the hallway was always very shy around me and seemed too frightened to talk or return my smiles and waves. I never heard a peep out of her until one night, she knocked on my door. I opened the door and she stood timidly in the dim light of the hallway looking at me with earnest and friendly eyes.

"There's a spider in my room," she said. "Will you kill it for me?"

My jaw dropped. Then I couldn't help but chuckle. "What makes you think I kill spiders?" I asked. "I'm a vegetarian; I love all living creatures."

Her face fell. "I … uh …," she began. Then the rest spilled out in a rush. "I figured that since you tell fortunes you must be into all sorts of spooky Halloween stuff and … maybe … oh, I don't know … " She looked up at me balefully. I imagine she thought I might like to throw the spider into a cauldron and cast a spell.

I went into her room and she pointed out the offending arachnid, which was still lying on her bedspread. Gently, I captured it in a drinking glass, carried it down the three flights of stairs, and released it into the bushes outside the dorm hall. She followed me sheepishly and grinned. "Thanks," she said. "I'm sorry I implied you were evil or bad or something. What is it that you really do?"

Thus began one of my most satisfying exchanges with a layperson that would alter another's perceptions about clairvoyance; many would later follow. You don't have to make a huge effort to promote clairvoyance, even if you believe it has changed your life. In fact, the best thing you can do to advance the cause is to make an effort not to shy away from intrusive questions and curious eyes.

Being clairvoyant is a big responsibility but it also comes with great blessings. When you are clairvoyant, a whole new world of sensory experience can open to you. The past and the future can seem more accessible and even better, more changeable. Best of all, you may be able to see some people whom you dearly miss, if distance or even death has separated you.

Imagine being able to see true visions of the past, present, and future with your own eyes. You can have the gift of powerful psychic vision, and it will feel natural and normal. Forget those movies where a clairvoyant doubles over in pain or shock, wincing because of terrifying premonitions. Clairvoyance can be a source of gentle wisdom, the sort of message that appears to you while sipping a cup of tea, rather than one the universe can deliver like a whack over the head with the "clue-by-four."

Clairvoyance ("clear-seeing") is the ability to see literal or symbolic truth using your eyes or the mind's eye. Being labeled psychic unfortunately carries with it certain expectations. It implies that you know everything. However, psychic perception simply means that you receive information through senses other than your usual five. Yes, you see with your eyes, however most of the perception of light that enters your eyes is actually processed and made useful in your brain. Thus clairvoyance, like physical eyesight, is something that is mostly performed by your brain. However, it also has a special link with spiritual ability. Think of it like your physical eyesight is governed by your body and your mind, while your clairvoyant sight is regulated by your mind and your spirit.

This book is designed for the beginner. With it, you will be able to learn how to experience clairvoyance on your own terms. Whether you've been struggling all your life to control your ability to see flashes of visions or you've never seen anything more than what's in front of you, you'll be able to develop your natural talents and potential abilities. We'll start with honing ordinary powers of observation. The natural world is full of omens waiting to be noticed and put to use.

When you're ready to move on to seeing things that are out of the ordinary, you can start with your eyes closed. The world of dreams is the best place for any budding psychic to start understanding the strange symbols and vibrant landscape of clairvoyant thought. Besides, you've probably already been dreaming all your life. Once you start gaining mastery over the understanding of dreams, you can then develop the ability to meditate and even go into a trance to see things in your mind's eye the same way you experience dreams.

For those brave enough to move on, you'll be able to start being clairvoyant with your eyes open. Tools that inspire your eyes and your subconscious, called scrying tools, serve as simple focus objects, like a bowl of water, crystal ball, or candle. By providing nondescript imagery or a blank slate, scrying tools invite your eyes and your mind to fill in the blanks with other things. Just as in your dreams, things that you see may be very symbolic, or you might find an emerging talent for seeing the literal past, present, or future.

Moving forward, you will be given tools for removing crutches for (and barriers to) psychic development while still keeping healthy boundaries. Once you're fully equipped to perform clairvoyant readings for yourself, you may want to do readings for others. You can learn to use your newfound clairvoyance to read people and advise on matters of love, money, career, and family. Finally, we'll get into the theory of clairvoyance, and we'll learn how to tell the difference between seeing spiritual visions…and being a candidate for the loony bin.

You're about to embark on an unusual journey for people in our modern culture. For most of us, seeing things that "aren't there" is something to be feared and is often misunderstood. As you approach clairvoyance seriously, you'll find yourself in a new world of ethical and spiritual issues. It is up to you to build a structure of moral, realistic, and socially conscious behavior when taking on the life-changing role of a clairvoyant. The life can be exciting, exhilarating, thought-provoking, and theologically inspiring. You'll need to know when to keep your eyes open and your wits about you. You'll need to be able to relax and close your eyelids to the world. This book is designed to empower the capable and clairvoyant you.

How to Use This Book

This book was written with the complete beginner in mind, so that even someone who has never had a clairvoyant vision will be able to develop that ability. To that end, skills are taught in a specific sequence to ensure smooth transitions. For example, you'll go from comfortable, everyday practices like observation and dreaming to more advanced techniques like seeing spirits and interpreting visions. It is important not to skip around in this book, even if you want to jump ahead to a more interesting part.

However, if after reading the first two chapters you have attained a certain level of clairvoyant practice, it is okay to read on past that level. You can apply the skills you learned while examining your dreams or meditating when figuring out how to interpret symbols (explored in chapter 5). In short, you don't have to push yourself beyond where you feel comfortable, but by all means go ahead and learn what is in store for you. Build at your own pace to more advanced levels.

one

Getting Started

Perhaps you've already had some psychic flashes—brief images in your mind of a future event that later came to pass. You may believe it was déjà vu or your mind playing tricks on you. You might not believe that you are a naturally talented psychic, or you may simply yearn to have moments of insight and intuition that can empower your life. No matter your level of experience, confidence, or ambition, you can start with some basics.

I've tried to remember my first clairvoyant experience, but honestly, I can't! When I was a child, I didn't just have an imaginary friend, I was constantly co-creating myself along with entire imaginary worlds. When I would tell my parents about visions I saw, they did not simply ignore a child's ramblings. Instead, they paid attention and encouraged my ability to see the world in a different way. When I had dreams that seemed to be premonitions about the future, my mother would smile and share some of her own, and she still does to this day. I don't believe my upbringing made me clairvoyant, however; it simply allowed me to begin developing my potential at an early age.

Everyone has the potential to be clairvoyant. Yes, even the grumpy old staunch atheist aunt in your family or the skittish and fearful young friend who can't even stand to think about the supernatural. Seeing is believing, and we all piece together our world from our perceptions, faulty or otherwise. Every one of us with normal, healthy physiology can't avoid making assumptions about our world based on information that comes into our brains in the form of visual cues as well as mental perceptions. The least creative person in the world still has dreams, and the most overactive imagination in the world can still tell the difference between an apple and an orange by sight.

When I was a very small child, my favorite soup was alphabet soup, and my favorite cereal happened to be one that was also made up of letters. I would screw up my eyes, think up a question, and then gaze into my bowl, hoping that the swirling letters I had moved with my spoon would give me an answer. They never disappointed me, but they were apparently expensive, and my parents preferred to purchase brand X cornflakes whenever we ran out. Undeterred, I continued to ask my questions of my cornflakes, gazing into the milky mysteries of the floating, soggy shapes that stuck to the sides of the bowl. What were once letters became pictures, but I could still tell the story of my answers as easily as if I were reading them in a book. What I was doing was a childish form of scrying in a manner almost identical to the tea leaf reading I do for adults to this day.

Where should you begin developing clairvoyance amid the backdrop of cultural tendencies and confusing psychology? The best way to start is with the skills and abilities that you already have. You may be a seasoned psychic or maybe you've never had any experience ever; all the same, you will have to identify what you are working with. You have your eyes, brain, and potentially a spirituality as your first resources; it is time to assess the prominence and importance of each.

How to Tap Into and Strengthen Your Clairvoyant Potential

Everyone is born with clairvoyant potential, even those who have limitations of visual acuity or a tendency to avoid intuitive thinking. The difference between an amazing seer and somebody who has never experienced a psychic vision is that the former put a lot more time and effort into developing clairvoyant potential. Yes, some people stumble upon natural predispositions earlier than others, but the reaction to clairvoyance can affect its development. Some people recall being vividly imaginative and clairvoyant as a child but then losing that ability while growing up. The good news is that you haven't lost that special talent! It might just be hidden from you right now in the course of your busy everyday life.

Think about when you were a very small child. Did you have an imaginary friend? Did you see things in the dark or in the clouds in the sky that weren't "real"? How did the adults in your life react? Imagine how people would react if you carried those "childish" tendencies into adulthood. Would your loved ones be supportive? Annoyed with you? Worried for you? At some point you made a decision to ignore some of the sensory inputs and perceptions that were a big part of your life, and I'd like to assert that your reasons for doing so were largely cultural.

However, if none of the above sounds familiar, don't be discouraged if you have never had a clairvoyant moment. Not everybody can remember their childhood imaginings or even their dreams from last night. You might want to ask your own children, or children in your life, to share their stories about imaginary friends and make-believe things. This can inspire you to live a creative second childhood. And don't be intimidated by lack of belief in what you may or may not see. You don't have to have the whole world figured out in order to begin your exploration of clairvoyance. In fact, you can start tapping into your potential without having to sacrifice skepticism or critical thinking. The most important mental skills of a clairvoyant are the powers of careful observation, the ability to notice important things from the background noise of everyday life, and a strong memory recall.

Down-to-Earth Practices, Not Mysticism

Right now, we have sophisticated computer models that predict our weather for meteorologists to broadcast over various media. Think about an early human, millions of years ago, who had nothing but experience with the clouds to foretell the weather. How like magic it would seem to a prehistoric person if he or she heard how we generate predictions today, to say nothing of how we access them on screens in homes everywhere. It turns out that the mysterious forces of the weather have scientific underpinnings we can study and understand with careful observation, even though we might sometimes be wrong. It is my belief that someday the mechanics behind clairvoyance will be thoroughly explained by science. But, for now, like those prehistoric people, we have to work with what we can observe and be our own scientists.

Let's start with visual basics. It is natural for an individual to be able to see some things that other people can't. In fact, I've already mentioned that our brains do more work on what we see than our eyes do, making each person's worldview unique. When we look at things in everyday life, light bounces off of objects and into our eyes, projecting on the backs of our eyeballs where sensitive anatomy allows the light to send electrical pulses to our brains. Once the raw data of light hitting your eyes meets your brain, some very special magic happens: your brain processes the imagery, allowing the flashes of electric signals in your synapses to become shapes and colors. Most amazingly of all, your brain draws your attention to some things while leaving out other things so that you are able to make sense of the world and make judgments based only on the most useful information. Without your brain's filtering, you would be overwhelmed by all the information coming from your environment. There are many reasons a person might not see something that is really there: the light isn't reaching the eyes, the signal isn't reaching the brain, or most often, the brain ignores it.

How to Be Observant and Intuitive

The first step to tapping into your clairvoyant potential is to work on becoming more observant of your surroundings. When you are performing a clairvoyant reading, you will want to gain every piece of information you can during a session. But you've spent your whole life training your brain to ignore visual information. If you're sitting in a room, your brain is helping you to avoid being distracted by the light a lamp may be shining on you. Even if you saw all the light switches and electrical outlets, you may not know where they are or how many there are without looking again for that information. If you are outside, you can see that there are many leaves on a tree without counting how many you can see. You may not even notice if any of the leaves are, say, yellow until you ask your brain to look for the yellow leaves. Your natural processing has filtered out plenty of information already that is true in your reality. It would be overwhelming to completely turn off your filter, but to begin as a clairvoyant, you'll have to start paying attention to things you see which have meaning. For example, a clairvoyant might notice and find it meaningful if he looked at a clock in the morning and it said 11:11 AM and then later on in the day he saw a license plate that said "1ONE1" and later a phone number with 1111 as the last four digits. Patterns are important for intuition, and you'll learn more about the symbolism of numbers later in the book.

Number pattern observation exercise

Grab a notebook and try spending an entire day paying attention to all the numbers you see throughout your day. Don't forget your house number, the building number on your place of work, phone numbers you dial, the license plate number on your car, or any of the other numbers you see on a daily basis. Also record any numbers that catch your eye throughout your day. It could be the numbers on the clock, repeated glances at your calendar, even numbers entered into your microwave or the number of people who share your elevator or stop in front of you at a stop light. You don't have to work very hard to ascribe a meaning to each one yet. The point of this exercise is to notice whether any numbers keep reappearing to you on a particular day. Over time, you might notice that the number dominating a period in your life fades out and another number gains prominence.

Observing change exercise

It is hard to notice gradual change. We tend to let small changes blend into the background of our day if they are unimportant. However, it's possible that the filtering you do automatically can allow changes that should be noticed to fall by the wayside. Even changes in your own body go unnoticed if they change slowly enough. Your face may look much different than it did a year or even a month ago, but when you look at it every day in the mirror you aren't truly observing your face for change. Try this exercise, which relates to the art of palmistry, or reading the hands.

The features on your hands are not always permanent, and yet you see them every day probably without noticing small changes. Try sketching your hands at least once a month in an observation notebook. Make note of the depth and length of the lines, the presence or absence of any natural dots or blemishes, and even paper cuts. Over time, look for changes in your skin, the definition of your hands, and their surface markings. You may be surprised to notice minute changes over time that would have gone unnoticed right in front of your face. Developing the skills of noticing change and depicting it accurately in your sketchbook will help you learn to awaken skills any clairvoyant needs to recognize important sights.

Finding meaning exercise

Clairvoyants are a very diverse bunch of people. There are clairvoyants of all genders, race, and creed. But one thing that all clairvoyants have in common is the ability to make quick mental connections in order to find meaning in the images that they see. As a clairvoyant, not only will you be seeing fantastic visions, you will also have to carefully tell the story of those images in a specific order for them to make sense in life's context. You'll have to start training your brain to find meaning and make connections between imagery in your everyday life.

How do you notice sights that have meaning? You'll have to tap into that inner child who finds wonder and magic in the small and everyday things around you. This kind of attitude is why children often make better clairvoyants than adults. When you feel something resonate emotionally, or surprise your intellect, don't ignore it and push on with your life. Instead, make a mental note. If you see a face that appears in the knots of a tree, stop and study it. If your eyes catch the iridescence of a fly's wing, marvel at its beauty. Note the opening bud of a blossom that announces a change in the seasons.

Try this exercise:

Grab a pen and paper. Go outside. Allow your eyes to take in as much information as possible. Look for three things:

faces, beauty, and change. Looking for faces in things is a good exercise for your ability to visualize because human brains are designed to recognize faces, so we tend to see them on inanimate objects or in chaotic patterns as well as on real people. Searching for beauty lets you tap into your emotional resonance with the world around you, helping you to find meaning in the ordinary and increasing your intuition. Finally, trying to notice when things have changed is an exercise that hones your powers of observation, and it can convey lots of information about the past, present, and future.

Are You a Visual Learner?

Can you remember what position your significant other was standing or sitting in when you first met him or her? When you read something in a book and later want to find the information, can you remember where the part you're looking for was on the page? Are you able to learn a physical skill like knitting or drawing from watching a video or looking at a series of pictures? If you answered yes to any of those questions, you are a visual learner, with each question increasing the indication of the strength of your visual learning ability.

When I was a schoolteacher, I learned that most people who live in Western culture are primarily visual learners, and we structure our school system around viewing information. If you are a visual learner, you are lucky because you will pick up clairvoyant talents more easily, and working with your natural strengths will speed your development. If you are not a visual learner, you will be able to focus on working with visual learning as a foundational skill in order to become a strong clairvoyant without giving up before you even get started.

How to Become a More Visual Person

I am not a visual learner; I am an auditory one. I can recite my favorite movies' audio tracks from memory, but if you show me how to do a new skill on a video, there's no way I'll be able to master it! Yet, I can still work on my visual learning skills in order to improve my ability as a clairvoyant. Just because I don't have the innate draw toward imagery doesn't mean I am unable to develop advanced talents through dedication and hard work.

If you are not a visual learner, you may feel more frustration when you begin developing your clairvoyant skills. Learning any new skill is hard, and here you are learning a new way of learning! Luckily, learning in this manner is quite possible, otherwise there would be no point to getting an education in a school. In some ways, school is all about learning how to learn, and so is being a psychic. In order to force your brain to make new connections and see things in your mind's eye more clearly, you'll have to practice visualization in your mind's eye, through drawing, and by starting to keep a record of things that you see.

What is visualization? When you were a child, you most likely had an active imagination. Of course when you looked at things, you saw them as they were, but you also had a playful version of people and objects that existed only in your mind. Visualization is the skill of mentally constructing a visual image using your imagination. Visualization can be playful, but it isn't merely a flight of fancy or a pretense, because in clairvoyance it can be used to see important truths. Visualization is also used by some psychologists in order to help people work towards their goals of being mentally healthy by imagining themselves and their lives as they want them to be. Treat your visualization exercises as though they are wishes that can actually come true.

Making a vision board

A vision board is a work of art made to depict your mental visions of what you want to have happen in your life. Constructing a vision board is a valuable exercise for a clairvoyant because it helps you express your hopes in visual form, an act that trains your brain to work visually for other clairvoyant exercises. Additionally, it allows you to start thinking of your destiny as something you are creating, rather than something that only happens to you through random circumstance.

To create a vision board, you'll have to think of an area of your life that needs improvement. Next, collect images from magazines or print pictures from the Internet of things you would like to see in your future. Make a collage to inspire yourself to work toward your goals, and place your collage in a prominent place as a reminder of your intentions.

1. *New home vision board:* If you are looking to buy a house, for example, paste some maps of desirable locations as the base of your vision board. Look for pictures of houses you like or ones that feature details of your desired home. For example, you might include the mascot or logo of the school district you'd want to be in, or bus stops to represent proximity to mass transit. If you love bay windows, hardwood floors, and purple paint, you can find those images to include. You can even add furniture and pictures that represent your family's happiness and relaxation in your new home.

2. *Love vision board:* Think about the good qualities you want in a partner, and then cut those images out of magazines to make a collage. Sure, you might cut out appealing body parts, but this exercise will help you think symbolically as well. What pictures might represent sweetness and kindness or other attributes you would desire in a mate? If you want a creative partner, you might include pictures of hobbies that such a person might enjoy. Don't forget to include images that represent how you will feel when you are finally together with the perfect mate.

3. *Weight-loss vision board:* Cut out images of outfits you might like to wear once you've reached your ideal weight. See if you can find photos for your collage of exercise activities you will enjoy on your route to fitness and afterwards. If you have a reward in mind after you reach your goal, include some photographs that represent your reward. For example, plan a trip to Hawaii and cut out pictures of sandy beaches and palm trees. I know it may be tempting to cut out pictures of supermodels in fashion magazines, but the truth is that the photos you see of what appear to be naturally perfect people have been digitally manipulated in very subtle ways. The goal of this vision board is to make you healthier—*not* skinny or rippling with muscles no matter the cost. Your health should be at the core of a vision board like this, not a particular pant size or number on a scale.

By now you probably get the idea, so you can make a vision board for any goal, including a new career, starting a family, or getting a car. If you're not a very visual person naturally, making a vision board can be a good tactile way to bring about some visual thinking. It can be tempting to write down words to express your intentions, but I urge you to think of symbolic pictures instead; you want to increase your clairvoyant visualization ability.

Practicing visualization exercise

Teaching yourself to see more images in your mind's eye can help increase your visual ability. Start by looking at things with the intent to recreate them in your mind's eye. Begin by choosing a simple and familiar object, like your favorite mug. Memorize every aspect of the mug's visual appearance, looking at any design on the outside, any stains on the inside and any markings on the bottom. Become aware of its proportions and the way the colors look in the light. Close your eyes and try to recreate every aspect of the mug in your mind until it is so vivid you feel that you could reach out and grab it in the dark realm beyond your eyelids. Hold the image as long as possible.

Advance the practice by visualizing the cup turning in space so you can examine the top and bottom, handle and front. Try practicing with other objects and even locations, such as an entire room or a familiar outdoor spot. Remember that recreating all the details will be impossible, since you naturally filter out some visual cues. Don't beat yourself up if you are unable to perform such a difficult task. Instead, use this exercise to increase your skills from whatever baseline ability you have now. Each time you practice visualizing, try to add more detail. At first it may be hard to even remember how many chairs were at a table. But with practice, you'll find that you even surprise yourself with the level of detail you can capture in your mind's eye.

Making a Record

Keeping a record of your observations is vital because of how the brain processes and stores information. Not only do you not notice some things, but you often forget some important things after seeing them. Clairvoyance is an art, and it requires living in the moment and developing strong visual recollection. Much of what we see is simply a memory of a projection in time. Let me give you an example of what I mean. Think about the last meal you ate. Try to picture it in your mind. Obviously, you're not seeing any actual food or drink but only a memory of the visual representation. When looking at something right in front of you, like this book, close your eyes and try to visualize it for a moment. Again, you're not seeing the book but a memory of something you saw mere seconds ago. Everything you see in your mind's eye is an image of something that happened at some point in the past—something that projected an image to your eyeballs and brain. Every clairvoyant vision you have will be a memory. As time moves forward, those memories will start to degrade the instant you stop seeing the vision, and with clairvoyance it is no different.

Keeping a journal of meaningful sights can be vital to capturing information in the first place and to not losing information as your memories fade. Also, you'll learn later that clairvoyants often see images that are highly symbolic. Rather than figuring out the puzzle right away, you may want to record the information to analyze and figure out at a later time. When doing clairvoyant readings, consider making an audio recording of your observations. You can speak much faster than you can write, and oftentimes talking through what you see can help you understand your observations and any analysis.

Keeping a sketchbook exercise

Since clairvoyance is visual, the ideal way to keep a record of your clairvoyance is in a sketchbook. Don't worry if you are not artistically gifted. Like a journal, a psychic sketchbook is a personal record that is just for you to keep track of yourself. In fact, it helps if you don't put too much time into making your drawings into perfect art. A fast sketch will more accurately capture what you've seen. Just try to portray important details like general shapes and sizes of what you see, as well as any relationships to anything else, be it objects or people. Don't forget to make a note of colors, too. Personally, I tend to use colored pencils so I won't forget what colors I saw. And don't be afraid that drawing what you see during a clairvoyant reading will make it come true—you are receiving an accurate picture of your destiny so that you can be empowered to change what you see, if you choose to do so.

If you haven't already, get yourself some paper and a writing implement as you read further into this book. The beginnings of your clairvoyance sketchbook will help you move forward and to literally see your progress. Progress is important to notice, especially to a beginner. Maybe you'd feel frustrated if you read a book on clairvoyance and didn't become an amazing oracle within a few days. Give yourself some credit: record your first steps so you can look back at a later time and see how far you've come. The power of observation is a skill—if you don't use it, you'll lose it! No matter how far you choose to progress in this book and advance your clairvoyant skills, continue the simple observation of the mundane world in order to carry those skills forward and use them in more advanced clairvoyant experiences you may pursue or stumble upon later in life. Grab your clairvoyance sketchbook and start it by writing out or sketching the exercises in this chapter. Here are a few more questions to think about and record your answers.

Getting Started Questions

1. Have you ever had any psychic moments in your life? Share a story about when your intuition surprised or helped you, or share a true ghost story.

2. What are your greatest hopes and dreams in becoming a clairvoyant?

3. What do you believe may be obstructing your clairvoyant practice?

Being Clairvoyant— Eyes Closed

Starting your clairvoyant journey with your eyes closed is a pretty good idea for a beginner. If you've already had clairvoyant experiences, closing your eyes and taking baby steps before allowing yourself to see things lucidly with your eyes wide open is a good safety measure to keep you feeling in control and not overwhelmed. If, to your knowledge, you have never experienced any clairvoyant visions, beginning with your eyes closed can help you develop basic skills and gain confidence so that you don't run into a roadblock of skepticism.

When people ask me how to get started with clairvoyant psychic development, I always say to start with your dreams; hopefully you already have plenty of experience dreaming.

While dreaming, it doesn't matter if you see scary or uncomfortable sights, because you know that after you wake up, you are safe and sound and that the world you saw in your dreams cannot interfere with your waking life. With that firm boundary between sleeping and consciousness, dreams are an excellent sandbox in which to play with your subconscious and with symbols that can have meaning for your life.

Your first step will be to put a dream journal by your bed along with a light and writing implement. Warn anyone else who sleeps in your bedroom that you will be writing in your dream journal if you wake up in the night. The hardest part about keeping a dream journal is to commit yourself to actually writing down your dreams upon waking. The details of dreams fade quickly in your memory upon waking, so no matter how much you may promise yourself that you will remember a dream the next day, some details will be lost.

It is much easier to roll over and go back to sleep, but for a clairvoyant, dream journaling needs to be undertaken as a serious task, as much as a priest might value the practice of prayer, or a body builder might be devoted to a morning weightlifting routine. All you need to do is to write out as many details as you can, being especially sure to write down the nouns; the people, places and things in your dreams. Date your entries, but you can choose whether you want to arrange them in chronological order, or keep the pages loose for a binder so that they can be organized more thematically.

Periodically, you should review your dreams. I tend to remember my dreams frequently due to practice, so I like to review them at least once a month so that I am not overwhelmed by the amount of material to go through. As a beginner, you may start out by not remembering quite as many dreams, so you may need to review your dreams every time you change your clocks, twice a year, or once a year on your birthday or New Year's day. If you dream prolifically, you might want to study your dreams weekly. Put it on your calendar.

When I study my dreams, I like to first go through and circle the symbols, which are usually nouns. As I do so, I keep a tally on a page in the front to see how many times specific symbols appear. For example, a strange woman, my husband, or a dog might appear in my dreams far more often than a shark or a volcano. The more frequently appearing symbols may be more important and meaningful in your life. The symbols may appear in different dreams, for example, seeing a dog in a dream about jogging in the park and then seeing another dog in a dream about a movie. Symbols can also repeat themselves in recurring dreams that play over and over again for you until you get the point.

For example, when I am stressed out, I have a recurring dream that my teeth are falling out. The first time I started having this recurring dream, I made sure to make an appointment with my dentist to get my teeth checked out, but they turned out to be healthy as usual. After recording this dream several times and noticing that the dream only happened in times of stress, I figured out what the dream meant to me symbolically. Losing teeth to me means a loss of control over my life. When I feel stressed, I feel out of control, leading to the dream.

If when reading my dreams I see a dream-event happen later in real life, I highlight that event with a highlighter. For example, I've seen a new person in my dream and then later met that person in real life. Of course, you won't be able to verify precognitive dreams until after they happen, but you will learn to enjoy the delicious déjà vu experience and run back to your dream journal as soon as possible afterwards. Those highlighted precognitive dreams can be analyzed for a pattern of timing. For example, if you notice that the events always come to pass within three days of your dream, you can set about trying to modify your actions if you want to prevent an event from occurring.

My mother has noticed that her prophetic dreams often come true within three days, and has taken to searching the news for stories that match when she dreams about big events. I remember one time we were driving together and she couldn't relax because she had a dream about a crumpled red car three days prior. "Watch out for that red car," she would say, "he's not driving carefully!" She figured that we might get into an accident. When we finally did see a red car on the side of the road that had gotten into a little fender bender, she breathed a sigh of relief.

Vivid Dreaming

Vivid dreaming is when you have especially visual dreams that occur in color. You may be a naturally vivid dreamer, or it could be that your dreams are not very visual at all. Just like being a visual learner, there are ways that you can increase your ability to dream vividly. Of course, the first way I recommend is keeping your dream journal religiously. By honing your powers of dream observation, you will find that you remember more and more visual detail. In turn, your brain will produce more vivid, colorful dreams.

There are those who make herbal dream teas in order to increase their vivid dreaming ability. I have had successful experiments with mugwort and wormwood teas, but in all honesty there is no herbal or drug replacement for making an effort to remember and record your dreams. By developing your ability to do these things, you'll naturally have more vivid dreams. If you skip this step when using herbal dream enhancers, you may not experience the full benefits. Herbs are real medicine, as well, so there is always the possibility of side effects to take into consideration.

Another safe way to enhance dreaming is to abstain from any sort of herbs, drugs, or alcohol. Restricting your food intake for the day and making sure that you go to bed on an empty stomach can make your dreams more vivid and potentially prophetic. Of course, make sure that you have permission from your doctor before restricting calories, and don't try it if you are pregnant or nursing.

If you find yourself not remembering any dreams, or if you believe you don't dream at all, try taking a vitamin B supplement and visiting your doctor. If the inability to remember your dreams goes along with an inability to get a full and restful night of sleep, you might have a sleep disorder that doesn't allow you to drop fully into the REM stage of sleep associated with dreams. Dreaming is important for everyone, not just those of us who want to learn clairvoyant techniques. Make sure you are getting good rest to have sweet dreams.

Lucid Dreaming

Lucid dreaming includes dreams in which you know you are dreaming and can interact with the dream's flow and content. It might seem counterintuitive to try to alter your dreams if you want to have a clairvoyant vision, but lucid dreaming can help you ask questions about the visions while you are still having them. Think of lucid dreaming as a sort of psychic sandbox where you can play out a potential past, present, or future.

Knowing that you are dreaming during a dream is a tough skill to learn, and even though I work on it myself, I still have many dreams after which I am surprised to wake up and realize I was asleep. Don't beat yourself up if you can't figure out how to interact with your dreams while you are having them; dreams in which you take a backseat to your subconscious are still very useful for the purposes of clairvoyant development.

A good beginner technique for attempting lucid dreaming is to repeat an affirmation before you go to sleep. Say something to yourself like, "I will be aware as I sleep," or "I have control over my dream life." Keep it short and sweet. It should be something like a mantra you can repeat over and over under your breath as you inhale and exhale. The trick is to keep repeating it as you fall asleep and continue until you lose consciousness. You may find this practice easier if you wake up in the night or early morning. Begin repeating the affirmation again as you drift back to sleep.

Be aware that lucid dreaming is quite a bit more difficult for the beginner than vivid dreaming. What makes this difficult is that your awareness of dreaming may pull you awake.

A few nights of such repeated waking can make you give up in favor of restful sleep, and that's okay. You don't have to torment yourself in order to be a lucid dreamer. The frequency of your attempts is more important than your intensity or your degree of success. So if you find yourself losing control and flying off into dreamland unawares, remember that there's always another night.

Using your dreams exercise

Once you establish a routine of recording your dreams, you can begin to use them for your purposes as a clairvoyant. Right now, your dreams work to process the events of your waking life and the feelings in your subconscious. This is done largely without your control. However, you can influence your dreams to help you answer a question or get advice from your subconscious. You can breathe normally without conscious effort or concentration, but you can slow or quicken your breathing at will. The same principle can be applied to bringing your dreams under control to work for you. Since your dreams exist entirely in the symbolic world, it is thought that they obtain the benefit of your psychic abilities. Some even believe that dreams are a way to cross over to the spirit world, where beings or deities can directly administer their aid.

Try this exercise only after you are confident that you can remember and record important dreams when you awaken. Allow yourself a very long preparation on the night of your important dreaming experiment. For example, switch off all screens and turn the lights down low or use candles to prepare your brain for sleep. You might want to drink a relaxing herbal tea and take a hot bath while you think up a topic of focus or a question that you would like answered in your dreams. Cleanliness has long been a technique used to make sure that the mind is blank and receptive to clairvoyant visions. Not only is a bath highly recommended, but you may wish to make sure that your bedroom is clean as well, with fresh, clean sheets on the bed. If your dreams seem especially convoluted or difficult to remember, go back and improve the cleanliness of your environment.

As you climb into bed and turn out the lights, focus your mind on the situation or question important to you. Keep asking the question or replaying the scenario over and over again in your mind visually as you fall asleep. If your mind wanders, immediately bring it back to the topic. You may find that this level of concentration makes it difficult to fall asleep, and that is okay. You will eventually relax into sleep, even if it takes a little bit longer. You'll also reap the benefits of a dream that can symbolically or literally show you advice. The more practiced you become with this technique, you'll find that it actually helps you to fall asleep faster and achieve a deeper state of sleep more quickly.

Trance Visualization and Meditation

While you are working on developing your dreams, you can simultaneously begin a daytime practice of meditation that can lead to trance visualization. Both techniques will be explained in detail, as they are vital to a clairvoyant practice.

Quiet and receptive meditation is the practice of clearing your mind and allowing sensory perceptions to come to you without analysis. Trance visualization is a technique of allowing your brain to drop into a trance, similar to the state you may be in right before you go to sleep or just after you wake up. During these times, it is possible to control your visualizations while allowing them to drift out of control in your subconscious as well, very much like dreams.

The benefit of doing these techniques is that they are like dreaming while being awake. You will naturally have more control over your experience while keeping a comfortable boundary between your time spent working on clairvoyance and your everyday waking life. For some people, the experience of meditative clairvoyance is like watching a television screen, but for others it can feel more subconscious or obscured. If you aren't yet ready to see things while you're awake, you can keep working on your dreaming until you feel more safe and familiar with the idea. There are some basic skills that should be worked upon for meditation, however, and those skills take time.

I suggest beginning with the first two practices: grounding, as well as an ongoing practice of quiet and clear-minded meditation. Not only are all of the other practices based on these two techniques, but they both take time and experience to learn. Both techniques are also gentle and not scary to those who may be a little leery of experiencing clairvoyance firsthand. The exercises after the first two are ordered for the beginner; they become more advanced as you gain skill and practice.

Grounding

Grounding is an energetic practice. When I talk about "energy" in the context of this book, I am not talking about the energy you learn about in science class. Rather, I am talking about the idea of *chi*. Chi is a life force that permeates the universe and all things within it. When you feel jittery and unable to sleep, you have more than enough of this form of energy. When you feel drained and unable to concentrate or stay awake, you have too little energy. The purpose of grounding is to balance out the energy in your body so that you feel both awake but also calm and ready to undertake mental and spiritual activity. There are many ways to ground yourself, but I will be focusing on visualization techniques for grounding, as you are developing visualization skills anyway.

Discovering your personal grounding visualization exercise

I will start with the ideal, which is the discovery of your own visualization, and then follow with a few example exercises for you to try. Pick a day to begin exploring grounding, and set aside some times of day that you know you will already be in different energetic states. For example, you may try morning, lunch time, and just before bed at night to observe your energy pattern. At each of these times, perform the same exercise.

Seat yourself and close your eyes. Check in with your body and mind to see how you feel. Are you groggy? Jittery? Exhausted? Unless it is the best day of your life, chances are you can imagine an improvement in your state of being, and unless you are having the worst day of your life, you have probably seen darker days. Try to visualize your internal energy as a pattern of light, color, or objects. Again, I will give you examples in a moment, but it is best for you to invent your own visualization, since it will be more personal to you and most accurately reflect what is actually going on inside your body. Note where the visual representation begins and ends. Is it contained within your body or does it extend further away from you? Are the boundaries fuzzy and unclear, or are they crisp? Is the visual representation of your internal energy in motion? Are there places where the energy seems stuck? If you see colors or lights, note where they are brightest and where they are dark. Sketch a representation of what you visualize in your clairvoyance sketchbook.

In order to complete this experiment, you should have several drawings in your sketchbook that depict your body in different energy states, flagging, enthusiastic, or anywhere in between. Once you do, you can work to shift your energy state through visualization. If your energy is feeling low, close your eyes and take note of how your energetic state appears to you. Then, by drawing energy up from the earth below you, replenish your energy—change the visualization so that it looks more similar to how your internal energy pattern appears when you are feeling more energetic. This will take time and practice; this level of visualization is difficult to sustain with concentration, and you may overcorrect at first and change your energy state to something you don't want.

Keep practicing at least once a day, as a beginner, to increase your skill and speed of visualization and grounding. As a proficient user of grounding methods, I can't even count how many times a day I ground myself, but I certainly do so before and after every clairvoyant exercise and also in times of high emotional stress. As you continue, you'll find that grounding becomes more automatic and can happen more efficiently. Don't worry if takes a long time to ground at this point, or if you seem to have not completed the process. Your skill and speed will increase naturally over with only diligent effort.

Grounding visualizations are highly individual, but many people have established common visualizations over time that work for many people. Although I encourage you to develop your own, I've provided some examples for those who feel stuck or for those who want to see how varied visualizations can be. You don't have to try all of these exercises and you don't even have to vary your own practice. Pick one that works for you and stick with it.

Grounding visualization example: tree

When Ria uses a grounding meditation, she chooses to visualize a tree growing inside her body. Sitting down on the floor in her apartment, Ria first imagines roots growing out of her lower body and feet, digging down into the earth. Even though she is not on the ground floor, she visualizes those roots snaking quickly through the ceiling and walls of the building, through the foundation and plunging deep into the cool, dark earth below. Her roots extend so deep into the earth that they reach for its molten core. She can see the base of her tree so strongly that Ria feels like she couldn't stand up and walk if she tried.

Next, Ria visualizes her body as the trunk of the tree and branches springing forth out of her head, reaching for the sky. Ria has already had a long day at work, and she feels mostly exhausted. She visualizes her tree roots drawing energy from the earth like water and nutrients for a tree. When she feels full of refreshing earth energy, she lets any excess negative energy from her day, like stress, burst forth from her head like the leaves from the tree, releasing the energy harmlessly up to the sky to float away from her. When she feels contented, Ria withdraws the visualization back into her body, seeing the roots vanish back up into her feet and the branches curl back into her head and then rests a bit before standing up and going about her day.

Grounding visualization example: chakras

Amit uses chakras as a way to ground himself. Chakras are places in the body where the energy pools and stirs. There are many different chakra systems that use differing numbers of chakras, from those that can be counted on the fingers of a hand to those that are infinite. Amit uses a system of six chakras. He seats himself cross-legged on a pillow in his meditation room and starts from the ground up. First, he visualizes a red ball of light at the base of his spine. Next, an orange ball of light a few inches up at his groin lights up. Amit visualizes a third chakra activating, at his belly, this one yellow. A rainbow of lights is turning on, like an elevator activating and energizing his body. His fourth chakra is green and lights up at his heart. The fifth is at his throat, glowing blue. The final chakra that Amit uses is right in between his eyes on his forehead, and glows a vibrant purple.

Keeping his focus on the rainbow of lights in his body, Amit views them critically, to see how they differ from usual. Normally, Amit finds that they are about the same size and vibrancy. Today, however, he finds that the one at his throat is more dim; darker and smaller than the rest. It makes sense to Amit that his throat chakra isn't doing so well. It rests about where his voice box exists, and he has felt ignored all day in his relationship with his wife. It seems like he needs to find his voice to reconnect with her. Amit visualizes the chakra at his throat growing and glowing brighter. When he feels satisfied that all of his chakras are even, Amit opens his eyes, ready to continue his evening with his family. Though some people go through the chakras and close them again in meditation, Amit likes to keep his activated and running throughout his quality time with wife and kids.

Grounding visualization example: fluid

Tricia likes to visualize water inside her body as a way to ground herself, because it is free-flowing. Liquids of any sort can be visualized for grounding, even swirling incense smoke. However, Tricia likes to picture water because she often feels too jittery and anxious, and loves to visualize all that excess negative energy pouring into the earth as she stands.

To start, Tricia finds a calm place in her home. She chooses her bedroom. She closes the door and locks it so that her kids and husband won't burst in and startle her. She turns off her cell phone, too. Tricia closes her eyes and imagines that she is filled completely with water. In fact, some of the water splashes up and outside her skin in waves. She can tell that she's still amped up from a busy day running around doing errands. Tricia regards the image in her mind's eye critically. The water in her body is mostly clear, but with frothy white waves splashing and a whirlpool in her head. There is a dark, still pool of water in the center of her chest.

Tricia visualizes the water flowing downward like a river, dripping down out of her feet as she stands upright in her bedroom. In her mind's eye, the waters calm so that there are no more splashing white tips extending outside of her body. As the water flows downward, the whirlpool in her head calms and joins the flow of the rest of the water. Tricia pauses to reassess her visualization. Now, in her mind's eye, all of the water is calm inside her body. In fact, the dark pool at her chest is still a little too calm. Tricia draws some energy up from the earth, visualizing fresh energy wicking up into her body like water into a paper towel. The still water in her chest stirs and joins the rest of the flow. Tricia feels calmed from her exciting day, healthy and ready to face the world.

Quiet and Clear-Minded Meditation

I'm going to admit something now: quiet and clear-minded meditation is boring. I'm saying that right away because I think the expectation that meditation will be a deep, spiritual experience right away is what turns off most beginners. Regardless, this type of meditation is the gateway to all other waking clairvoyant practices. Without being able to clear your head of your busy everyday life to tune in to your clairvoyant visions, you'll be a distracted and inattentive psychic at best. Once you've mastered the boring part, you'll be able to move on to receiving clairvoyant visions, entering a trance state, and other psychic practices.

As a bonus, you should also know that this type of meditation has health benefits such as lowering blood pressure and reducing stress. So, since you will have to start practice without any immediate, amazing clairvoyant reward (just remind your-self that your health is improving). Hopefully that will give you enough motivation to continue to learn to master your own mind.

Start by reducing all your distractions and making sure you won't be disturbed in any way during your meditation. If you're a beginner to meditation, give yourself a very short goal, like five minutes. If you are unsuccessful, you can make it shorter. I'm naturally inattentive, so my first successful meditation session was a whole thirty seconds. If you're like me, it might be a good idea to set a timer so you won't be constantly peeking at a watch or a clock.

Seat yourself comfortably, but not so comfortably that you'll fall asleep. You might have to practice several times a day to find out what time is easiest for you to meditate. Some people find that first thing in the morning is best, but I end up nodding off. I prefer late evening or afternoon meditations. Close your eyes and clear your mind. Yes, this is the hard part. If thoughts bubble up in your mind during this type of meditation, don't berate yourself; it is normal. Just observe them as if you were an outsider, without building on the thoughts. Let them float away just as they came. Practice this meditation daily, extending the period of time in which you meditate by a few minutes at a time until you can meditate at least thirty minutes. Thirty minutes is a reasonable goal for a beginner, but don't be surprised if it takes years to accomplish.

There are a few tricks to keeping a clear mind. They all have to do with staying inside your body and in the present moment instead of letting your mind wander. Paying attention to your breathing or heartbeat is one way to focus on something during meditation without compromising a clear head.

Choose your breathing, for example, and just breathe naturally while focusing all of your attention on your breaths so that the only thing you are thinking about is the in and out of oxygen. You can also choose your heartbeat, and touch your fingers to your wrist or neck to sense your pulse as you meditate. Drive all thoughts from your mind except the rhythm of your heart.

The purpose of the heartbeat or breathing focus in this form of meditation is to get yourself settled. Like an eraser to a blackboard, your focus will allow you to erase intrusive thoughts. You may find that you don't need these crutches, and that is okay. In fact, for the next type of meditation, you'll likely need to phase out your attention on your heartbeat or breathing in order to pay attention to other things.

Entering a Trance

Trance meditation is a step above and beyond simple quiet meditation in which you clear your mind. The goal of trance meditation is to enter a different brainwave state, the alpha wave state, which is where your brain rests. Usually you enter this place just about to fall asleep or just about to wake up. There are countless ways to induce a trance state, from drugs to pain to sex to religious rituals. Some may be able to enter a trance simply by practicing quiet meditation as described earlier. For the beginner, however, I'll include two other methods, breath control and dance.

You can allow your breathing to occur naturally and observe it, but you can also control your breaths to relax into a trance state. Breathing in through your nose and out through your mouth achieves this. You can also slow your breathing by feeling your heart rate and then breathing in for four heartbeats, holding your breath for four heartbeats, breathing out for four heartbeats and holding again for four heartbeats. This kind of breathing is called square breathing, and if you link it to your heartbeat, you'll find that both your breathing and your heart rate slow together, bringing you into a more relaxed state.

How do you know when you've entered a trance? You may find yourself advancing naturally to receptive meditation, and dreaming while wide awake. You may simply find that your body functions slow to the point where you wouldn't be able to jump to your feet and run after completing the meditation. It is important to let yourself readjust slowly after any meditation session, since your blood pressure may drop and your brain may enter a dream state, making your coordination a little impaired.

Practice breath control techniques—add them to your daily meditation until you can enter a trance state and then phase out the breath control without disturbing your relaxation. After your brain begins producing that alpha wave state, you don't have to keep concentrating on your breathing. You can release your focus and clear your mind so that you are both in a trance state and also in that quiet and clear meditative practice that you began before.

If breath control just isn't working for you, or if you would like to add another trance practice to your repertoire, you can try trance dancing. Select some music you can play while you meditate. There's a variety of trance-specific music available, or you can choose drumming music, the traditional choice in many cultures. Drum tracks are especially effective if the drumming is at about the same rate (beats per minute) as your pulse. Music without words works best. Personally, I have difficulty entering and maintaining a trance with music unless it is an instrumental piece, because otherwise I find my conscious brain paying too much attention to the lyrics.

Clear your dance space and adjust the lighting so you can see clearly enough without bright lights detracting from the mood. Yes, you can and should keep your eyes open while you are trance dancing. If you're clumsy like me, forgo the candles while you do this, so that you don't accidentally bump into a burning candle while dancing. Start slow, with small movements in place, attempting to keep a clear mind while you dance. As you become more comfortable with your movement, you may be able to circle around the room and move more quickly if desired, but you can stay in one place and trance dance just as effectively.

Try stomping your feet and clapping your hands. You don't have to look like an amazing professional dancer. The purpose of this sort of trance dance is not to take it to the floor of a night club. Instead, you're working to get your heart pumping and your brain leveling out into that alpha wave state. That said, you don't want to move too quickly unless you already have the stamina of an athlete. Keep your movements small and slow enough that you can maintain your dance throughout your meditation without having to take breaks. Once you are in a trance, see if you can slow and eventually stop your movements without disrupting your trance state.

Receptive Meditation

Receptive meditation is the next step after trance meditation. Make sure that you can reliably achieve a clear head and a trance before you move on to receptive meditation in order to get the best results. In receptive meditation, the goal is not to consciously populate your mind with ideas, but to allow psychic perceptions to come through from other sources than your waking brain. That means that as a beginner, you'll have to be practiced enough to get into a trance state and then relinquish any techniques you were using in order to pay full attention to what may come next.

To be a clairvoyant, you'll want to be able to see visions in your mind's eye without purposely putting them there. It will feel very much like dreaming while you are awake, as long as you are in a trance state. As a result, you'll need to grab your sketchbook so you can record the visions you see as soon as you are done with your receptive meditation session, otherwise you'll find that you forget them as easily and quickly as dreams can slip from your memory.

For receptive meditation, you'll have to go through the steps of all of the other techniques you have already learned. So, start out by preparing a space in which you won't be disturbed, and have your sketchbook and writing implement close at hand. Set a timer.

1. Ground yourself.

2. Begin quiet meditation and clear your mind.

3. Enter a trance. You can use techniques like breath control or dance.

4. Phase out any breath control or dancing while maintaining your trance state.

5. Maintain this trance, employing quiet and clear meditation as long as possible.

6. Record any visions that arise in your mind's eye immediately after you are done with your timed session.

If you don't see any visions in your mind's eye over the course of several practice sessions, it is time to do a little troubleshooting. The most likely culprit is haste. You may have to go back over your techniques and make sure you're not rushing through them. If you are taking your time and feel quite comfortable with the meditations prior to this one, you can try to omit grounding before your meditation session. If you omit grounding prior to meditating, your visions may be more forthcoming, but you will have to be sure to ground yourself very well afterwards, taking extra care and time so you don't encounter any of the sick feelings that result with a lack of grounding. Eating food can also be very grounding, so don't eat a heavy meal right before you try to meditate. Sometimes I will fast before meditating in order to increase its effects.

If you still have trouble seeing visions in your mind's eye, go back to the visualization exercises for increased visual learning in chapter 1. Your subconscious mind may just need a little help realizing what it is supposed to do during receptive trance meditation, so you'll have to practice visualizing for a while before resuming your practice. The point of these exercises is not to let an overactive imagination run wild or to make you worry about whether you're crazy. It may be frustrating, but these things take time. Remember that you've probably spent your whole life in a culture that believes "seeing things" is scary and bad—you may encounter some resistance from your own psyche. Slow progression is encouraged; develop your clairvoyance in a controlled way.

Controlled and Uncontrolled Visualization

In your dream practice, I asked you to try thinking about a problem or situation before falling asleep so you could encourage your subconscious to dream about the topic. You can use the same technique before a receptive trance meditation session. However, other techniques have been used to access certain topics in your subconscious. The most common technique is to visit a place in your mind; a landscape in which different areas represent different places that you can go for answers. You might meet people or animals along your way in the landscape who give you advice. The style of visioning in which one travels through a mental landscape is often called a spirit journey.

The mental landscape that you create is often called the astral plane, as it is a level of existence beyond the literal and physical one in which we are now present. There are many ways to get to the astral plane. Some people seem to simply find themselves there as soon as they drop into a receptive trance meditation. You can also travel there by first visualizing the room in which you are meditating. Like the exercise in chapter 1, you'll need to be very precise, creating every detail with your eyes closed in order to urge your brain to work visually. Then, you can travel to the astral plane any way you like. Here are some suggestions:

1. Visualize a door in the floor somewhere in the room. Open the door and fall through.

2. Let yourself fall or float upwards into the sky and find a new landscape.

3. Climb onto a rainbow elevator. Slowly let yourself travel up or down through all of the colors of the rainbow.

4. Find a long spiral stairwell in the room that travels up or down for a good distance.

The longer it takes you to journey to the astral plane, the deeper you may be able to go into your trance, so take your time. Once you get to your astral plane, it is a good idea to visualize a comfortable home base. Your home base will be the place you go any time you first travel to the astral plane or get ready to leave the astral plane. And, just like Dorothy in the *Wizard of Oz*, you can wish yourself back to your home base any time you desire.

I want to avoid building the idea of your home base *for* you, because it should be a place that personally feels beautiful and comfortable. A few quick suggestions are either a natural outdoor space or perhaps a childhood home. Either way, you should get to know your home base on the astral plane like the back of your hand. It is your controlled area, so if you encounter spirit people or creatures on the astral plane, you can ask them to leave your home base and they will. The first few times you travel to the astral plane, stay at your home base and familiarize yourself with the area.

In order to travel away from your home base, all you need to do is visualize labeled doors or paths leading from your home base. The labels can change whenever you wish. This is where you can transition from controlled visualization to uncontrolled visualization. For example, you can have doors labeled "my love life" or "my career" and walk through those doors to new and uncharted landscapes. Like dreaming while awake, everything you see when you walk through those specific doors will be advice for the topic at hand in symbolic or literal form. More about interpreting these symbols will be in chapter 5. For now, you can add the symbols you see to your sketch book.

As a beginner, you may feel some trepidation as you step away from consciously visualizing your home base and allow yourself to have uncontrolled visions outside of it. It can feel uncomfortable to be out of control while awake, and some people may be unable to relinquish control and as a result, see nothing new. It is important to take your time and to allow yourself to relax into those alpha wave states associated with the beginning stages of sleep, enabling you to effectively dream while awake. And don't feel frustrated if you don't understand your visions; let them happen and record them afterward for later analysis. Remember that you can wish yourself back to your home base and return to your regular life in the same way that you visited at any time.

Some people are afraid that they won't be able to return from the astral plane. You need not be concerned, but if you are, there are two ways that you can feel more secure. One way is to visualize a cord connecting your "astral self"—the image of you in your mind's eye that is traveling the foreign landscape —to your physical self, sitting or lying down at home. Some people visualize a bright umbilical cord connecting the belly buttons of both selves. The unbreakable cord can be followed back to wakefulness instantly, no matter what you see or where you go on the astral plane.

Another way to feel more secure is to hold onto a rock while you meditate. As you travel on the astral plane, you carry the rock with you. Whenever you want to return to your physical body, you need only squeeze the rock or turn your attention to it, and you will instantly return to your body. The rock acts as a symbolic and physical source of grounding, enabling you to ground the energy of your meditation quickly and safely, and return you to the physical plane.

Psychometry

Psychometry is a very special sort of clairvoyance involving objects. A clairvoyant can have visions that depict the object's importance and the things that happened with the object simply by holding it. For example, a skilled clairvoyant may be able to hold a murder weapon and be able to see visions of the crime. Psychometry can also operate on photographs. A talented clairvoyant might be able to hold a photograph of a missing child and be able to see the child's location or even the kidnappers. Anyone can develop psychometry, but it may take considerable time to achieve.

The first step to developing your psychometry will be to gather objects of yours you already know have meaning. The best objects for practice are ones that have been involved in one or more very emotional moments in your life. An engagement ring, a childhood comfort item like a blanket or stuffed animal, or an object that belonged to a loved one who is now deceased, a love letter or other memento from a passionate romance are all good examples. It is best to stick with one object at a time, so don't worry if you can't think of too many.

Take the object and examine it as many ways as you can. Look at all of its angles. Even smell the object and see if it has a detectable scent. Close your eyes, and while holding the object, recreate it in your mind's eye in as much detail as possible. Don't leave out a single characteristic. Allow yourself to feel any emotions associated with the object. Amplify those emotions in your mind so that the joy is more ecstatic or the sadness brings fresh tears to your eyes, if possible. Train your mind to go to your emotions as soon as you initiate psychometry.

If you have a natural predisposition to psychometry, you may begin to build scenery around your mind's eye of an important past event in the life of that object as soon as you begin to feel the emotions. If not, you can consciously build the scene from your memory, again trying to flesh out all the details. You will know whether your psychometry is progressing when you see more details whenever you make an attempt.

Psychometry with your own treasured memories can be very engaging, but try not to overwhelm yourself by switching from one object to the next very quickly. The point of these exercises is to visualize with depth and detail, and to condition your brain to go through the steps to show you as much information as possible. If you don't linger on this practice until you feel very comfortable and adept, you'll find yourself switching to other objects frustrating. Try to focus on one object a day at most in your meditation session. The best-case scenario would be to spend a week meditating with one object so you can build up an entire repository of visually experienced memories associated with it.

Next, gather some photographs of very meaningful moments to you. For this initial exercise, choose a picture in which you have been photographed. It can include other people as well. Remember that during meditation you will be studying only one photograph at a time. Begin by examining the photograph with your eyes open, taking in every detail. Memorize all of the colors and aspects of the photograph. Close your eyes and practice recreating the photograph in your mind's eye until you are confident you have a perfect memory of the picture. Allow yourself to feel the emotions of the memory depicted in the photo, and amplify those emotions as much as possible.

The next step is to visualize yourself inside the picture, standing in the same position you were in when the photograph was taken. This step is hard for people like me, who have difficulty with spatial thinking, so don't feel frustrated if it isn't easy. At this stage in your visualization, you'll have to recreate the memory of the scene in which the photograph was taken, including many details not pictured (for example, of the person taking the picture). Again, you'll know your skill is increasing when you visually remember more details. You don't have to force the scene to be frozen like the image; people and things can move in your visual memory, if you would like.

Spend a day or a week on one photograph so that you can get comfortable putting yourself in the photographic memory. Visualize as much as possible.

Try the photograph experiment with pictures of yourself at different ages. If it is going well, one way to progress your practice is to first put yourself into the photograph of yourself at a specific age, and then let yourself recall another visual memory from that age. Force yourself to relive the emotions and all the visual details. This isn't just ordinary daydreaming; you are training your brain to have a photographic recall of visual details. When you eventually move on to photographs of other people, you may want to have clairvoyant visions of them in scenarios other than one in which a photograph was taken.

To take your psychometry to the next level, get some volunteers to give you some meaningful objects and photographs from their own lives. Ask your volunteers not to tell you about the importance of the objects or photographs so you can attempt to use your clairvoyant ability to gather the details without too much conscious effort. Start with the objects. Why? It is believed that since the objects have been physically touched by the energies of important memories, they can most easily trigger clairvoyant visions in a beginner.

As with your own object, start by examining it with as many senses as possible and then recreating the object in your mind's eye. As you do so, pay attention to your emotional state. You may find that you begin feeling an unexpected emotion or an emotion that doesn't feel like your own. Since the emotion is the important part of this exercise and will trigger a clairvoyant vision rather than just an imaginative daydream, I encourage you not to move forward until you feel an emotion. If you do not feel an emotion, simply hold the object in meditation and then try a meditation again with the same object the next day.

Once you successfully start to feel an emotion while meditating with the object, amplify that emotion in your mind. Force yourself to get all worked up about it. It's okay if you inexplicably laugh or cry. Remember, you are in charge of this meditative session and your emotions. Our culture often teaches us that extreme emotions mean that we are out of control. However, the clairvoyant needs to be able to experience extreme emotions while remaining in control. As a beginner, you may need to fight against your cultural training or against your coping mechanisms, both of which are geared to repress extreme emotions.

While experiencing the strong emotion you've generated, try to allow the surrounding circumstances, environment, and people associated with the object to appear in your mind's eye. This part of the process can also be hard for beginners. You may wonder how much of what you visualize is consciously created in your mind as a flight of fantasy and how much is a genuine clairvoyant sight. One way to encourage more of the latter is to make sure that you are in a receptive trance during your meditation with the object.

If you still think that you are inventing the scene consciously, or if you have trouble visualizing a scene at all, there is another technique you can try. Hold the object; visualize it in your mind's eye. Feel the emotions and then transport yourself to your home base on the astral plane. Visualize a door or a path associated with the object that leads you out of your home base. Hopefully, this visualization prompt will help your brain start subconscious and uncontrolled dreaming so you can move away from forced, conscious imagination. Make sure that you sketch any visions that you have while meditating with the object no matter how silly or unlikely they seem. The things that you see may be symbols that make more sense to the volunteer that gave you the object. For example, I once saw a live turkey in a vision, which seemed like an awfully strange thing to see for a person who had just asked me about her ex-husband. It turned out that they had a significant emotional event on Thanksgiving that affected their relationship, and the turkey was a symbol for that event.

Working with photographs of other people can be more challenging than with objects. I am often asked whether a clairvoyant can use a digital picture of somebody. For many clients of my fortune-telling business, digital photography is all they have. Yes, the point of working with photographs is different than working with objects. If you use an old photograph that has been handled by a person in an emotional state, you may be using the photograph more like an object than a picture. For the next exercise, you'll be using the technique for photographs rather than for objects, so a digital picture, photocopy, or new print will work just fine, and in fact is good for making sure that you're improving a particular skill set.

Stare at the picture until you have memorized it and can picture it with your eyes closed. Try to place yourself inside the photograph as the person who gave you the photo. Search inside yourself for emotions and try to amplify them in your mind. If you see anything beyond the frame of the photo, make note and record those details immediately following your session. Making certain that you are in a trance can aid the process, as can a visit to your home base on the astral plane then leaving through a door or path labeled with the photograph in your mind's eye. Try to spend a week meditating with the same photograph before going to the person who owns it to try verifying any details you have recorded from your clairvoyant visions. Remember that the things you see might be highly symbolic, so even if they seem silly or unlikely, they may turn out to be meaningful for the person involved.

Psychometry of places

Don't forget that things like buildings are objects, too. You can practice your psychometry by going to new places and sensing things about them. Next time you visit a historical site, try closing your eyes and touching the walls or the floors, allowing yourself to sense the past and the emotions felt in that place just as you would with an object when practicing psychometry. In fact, you may find that it is easier and almost automatic to use your psychometry when inside a building. Psychometry might explain any spooky feelings you get when you are inside a place where bad things have happened.

When I have bought homes in the past, I used all my senses and clairvoyance in the form of psychometry when getting a feel for a place. As a clairvoyant, I am particularly sensitive to the energies of spaces, so it would not do me any good to live in a home in which terrible events have left their energetic imprint. In some cases, I have been in houses that didn't have anything objectively wrong with them, but I did not like the visions I saw flashing before my mind's eye when being inside them. In those cases, I trusted my intuition and moved on to find a different home that brought more pleasant imagery to mind.

Establishing an Eyes-Closed Clairvoyant Practice

As a beginner, I can't stress enough how being clairvoyant with your eyes closed is a complete and sustainable practice in and of itself, because I know some beginners are frightened of "seeing things" with their eyes open. The vast majority of clairvoyants stop at the practices in this chapter and can even build highly successful professional lives using just these techniques. If you just want to use clairvoyance for yourself, meditation and dream journaling are excellent exercises. They will help you build up your clairvoyant ability and allow you to have restful sleep and enjoy the health benefits of meditation.

If you want to do clairvoyant readings for a friend or loved one, it isn't so hard to say, "Let me dream about that and get back to you." Even many professionals will close their eyes and enter a trance in order to have clairvoyant sessions with their clients.

However, being clairvoyant with your eyes open is an advanced step that helps many people feel more fulfilled in their psychic practices. The reality of visions seems more imminent when not locked in a dream-like state. There are also those who may feel uncomfortable entering a trance on a regular basis, and some of the eyes-open techniques in chapter 3 can be performed not only in a trance, but also while fully conscious.

Exercises

1. Share an entry from a dream journal with a friend for interpretation.

2. Develop a grounding visualization. See if you can lead another person through a guided meditation to practice a grounding technique.

3. Have someone bring you an object and a picture to practice psychometry.

three

Being Clairvoyant—
Eyes Open

Being clairvoyant with open eyes is a much different experience. For one thing, these techniques can often be performed fully alert, so you can keep your wits about you and communicate what you see. You are also less likely to forget visions that can easily fade when obtained in a trance. Keeping your eyes open also makes clairvoyance feel more like an undeniable reality. In chapter 5, we'll go into how you can confront any reservations or concerns you may have about seeing things others do not. But if you feel bold and ready to experience the next level of clairvoyance, proceed with the exercises in this chapter.

Now that we have our eyes open, I'll start with transforming your observations of the natural world into an understanding of omens, which is a way to turn ordinary things into psychic symbols. Next, I'll go into several divination systems that are conducive to developing your clairvoyant abilities. Divination is a system of techniques and symbols to organize omens in a more workable way. Finally, you'll be able to graduate to seeing some clairvoyant phenomena with your own eyes that other people may not be able to see in the same way. Though the journey may be unusual, it will be safe and controlled. As you advance through the methods, stop whenever you feel uncomfortable or out of your element.

Seeing Is Believing

Since you'll be taking in some clairvoyant sights visually, the techniques in this chapter may alter your entire belief system. In particular, you may see some things that symbolically or literally predict your future or things that represent somebody you know who has died. For this reason, it is especially important to continue using your clairvoyant sketchbook to record your journey. If you start to modify your beliefs based on what you see, feel free to keep a written journal in your sketchbook as well so you can strengthen your beliefs. Your understanding of the world changes over time. Think about how different your view of the mind and spirit is from when you were a small child. Becoming a clairvoyant with open eyes will awaken you to a new world and accelerate your personal growth in a new direction.

Omens

Omens are ordinary events that are understood to be more meaningful through cultural psychic associations. As you continue honing your observation abilities (started in chapter 1), you may begin to notice that some things you see are more meaningful than others. You are already familiar with some of the most common omens. For example, you've learned that you are more likely to have a wish granted if you snap a turkey's wishbone and get the larger piece, or if you manage to blow out all of the candles on your birthday cake, or if you happen to notice the first star that becomes visible in the darkening night. Likewise, you've heard that walking under a ladder or breaking a mirror can be an omen of bad luck.

In addition to commonly known omens, you can start collecting your own. For example, if you notice a particular species of bird every time you buy a lottery ticket that wins a few dollars, you've discovered an auspicious omen for you. Write down and sketch these observations and associations in your clairvoyant journal so you can build an entire dictionary of omens for yourself. The following are some more common symbols.

bat: Although some cultures believe bats carry messages from the dead, and Europeans believed a bat circling the house three times was an omen of death, the Chinese believe that a bat is a sign of good luck when sighted.

birds: Birds in flight have traditionally portended good or bad luck, or yes/no answers to a question. A bird's flight from right to left across your field of vision can mean a yes or good luck, with a left to right movement meaning "no" or bad luck. Often owls are said to be reversed from the usual. However, traditional interpretations are often flip-flopped, so I recommend making your own observations and associations to see which directions of bird flight (and species) means a positive omen to you.

black cat: You've probably heard that a black cat crossing your path is bad luck as well, though black cat owners would heartily disagree.

broom: A broom falling over traditionally means that visitors are coming to your home.

double rainbow: Seeing a double rainbow is a sign of good luck.

penny: Finding a penny on the ground is a sign of good luck, particularly if it is heads-up.

red sky: A traditional folk weather prediction is that a red sky seen in the morning portends windy and stormy weather, while a red sky seen at night predicts clear and calm weather at sea.

In addition to making natural associations with omens (for example I tend to like bats and black cats and think that they are good luck rather than bad), you can also ask for an omen to be presented to you. Imagine, for instance, that you are walking out of a job interview and wondering if you got the job or even if that job is the right one for you. You can ask for an omen to be presented to you. For example, you might say, "May I see a squirrel running across my path today carrying a nut if this job is for me." If you happen to see such a squirrel, record the sighting in your sketchbook as soon as possible.

Even if you choose not to take the advice of the omen the first time you see it, keeping a record of the omens and their results will help you believe your eyes the next time around.

Divination Tools: Smoke and Mirrors

Omens are an exciting way to become more observant of the world around us. However, those special signs aren't always there when we need them. Often, the lack of an auspicious omen is the only hint we can get of a negative answer if the consequences aren't dire. After all, you wouldn't wait on and expect the universe to send you a hundred signs if you are trying to choose the best colors for your wedding. Divination, therefore, is the use of tools or techniques that can be consulted on the user's own time and terms.

Another limitation of omens is that they are often unclear. If you're trying to predict an answer based on whether a bird flies to the right or left and it flies straight over your head, what was the answer? Using a system of divination can allow you to ask the question in another way immediately, rather than needing to wait until another bird shows up. Although there are countless divination methods and systems, for the purposes of this book I will focus on those which increase clairvoyant ability by assisting visualization skills.

Scrying

Scrying is a divination method requiring a tool that is used to observe certain images that are interpreted as symbols. I will cover use of a few tools including incense smoke and scrying mirrors. The term "smoke and mirrors" is usually used in a context implying stage magic or performed illusions. In the case of scrying, however, these tools are to initiate your imaginative subconscious rather than to trick your brain into thinking you are seeing things. Your eyes actually *will* see shapes and other images that others can perceive. Your clairvoyant mind and emotions, however, will be able to attach meanings that can confirm past events, give advice about present situations, and even predict the future.

Crystal ball reading

Crystal ball reading is one of my favorite forms of scrying, partly because of its history connected with traveling fortune tellers and séances, and partly due to its ease of use for beginners. If you can see shapes in the clouds in the sky, you can perform a crystal ball reading. This type of scrying does require a small investment up front to buy a quartz crystal sphere, but it doesn't matter how small in size it may be. Please don't settle for a glass ball, because in order for a beginner to have successful crystal ball readings, the crystal needs to have small imperfections. These occlusions, often looking like rainbow-colored or shiny chips or shards floating inside the crystal, are natural deformations caused by time and pressure. It is those crystal flaws which will spark your imagination to see shapes, just like when children see shapes and meaning in the clouds in the sky.

Choose a crystal ball of any size, though smaller is usually more affordable. It is best to pick out a crystal ball in person from a metaphysical book store or a rock shop. Find one that has enough flaws in it to see something unique from every angle, but is not so cloudy or clear that you are unable to make anything of the small imperfections within. The other supplies you'll need are your sketchbook and a writing instrument. Good lighting is also key to using a crystal ball. You might want the dim lighting of candlelight for mood, but I prefer quality reading lamps. Watch out for sunlight, as it can act like a magnifying glass and burn your hand as it holds your crystal ball.

As a beginner clairvoyant, it is recommended that you meditate and enter a trance before working with your crystal ball. These are early days, so don't stress out if you aren't able to see things instantly the first time. Eventually, you may be able to gaze into it and see things without even using the trance state. But in the beginning, you may have to spend some time getting to know your crystal ball. The following steps may help.

1. Ground yourself.

2. Meditate and enter a trance.

3. Open your eyes and pick up the crystal ball, turning it slowly in the light until a sparkle from one of the inclusions catches your eye. Stop moving the crystal ball to examine it further.

4. Zero in on that one small feature within the crystal ball, and try to identify the shape that you see. Try not to move the crystal ball too much, or you may completely lose track of it. If you need to, carefully reposition the ball just a little to see more clearly.

5. Once you see a shape, note its color and any other surrounding shapes. Sketch and describe what you see in your journal.

At first you may only be able to see one thing in the crystal ball per session. Over time, however, you will be able to see more without forgetting, especially if you can get yourself to see things in the crystal ball without entering a deep trance state. When I do crystal ball readings now without a trance state, I usually see about ten different shapes per reading, turning the crystal ball in between sightings of shapes.

What are some of the shapes you can see? As a beginner, you may start out seeing very simple shapes such as hearts and stars. Count the numbers of objects you see, as the number may be meaningful as well. As you practice with your crystal ball, you will be able to see letters in a person's name and even peoples' faces or details of a location such as buildings, trees, and mountains.

In my experience with crystal ball reading, I've been able to see parts of road signs that helped people find missing pets that had run away. I've been able to see initials, uniforms, and facial features that have helped to identify people. And, I've been able to see features of houses and property that have identified locations as well. Aside from literal interpretations, most of my crystal ball readings are highly symbolic as well, giving messages in the form of pictures that have to be interpreted. More about interpreting images will be included in chapter 5. For now, write it down if an image immediately has a symbolic meaning that jumps to mind. If something doesn't make sense at all, it is good enough to sketch what you see for later review.

An entire book can be written on crystal ball reading alone, (and indeed I have written one myself). However, for the purposes of advancing your clairvoyant ability, it may be best for you to switch between different scrying methods so your brain gets used to picking out meaningful images in various media. Pretty soon, you'll be so well conditioned to see visions that you'd be able to scry in a toothbrush, no fancy crystal ball required!

Tea leaf reading

I love to recommend tea leaf reading to beginners, not only because it uses the same technique of picking out shapes as with clouds in the sky, but also because the ritual of preparing the tea and pausing to enjoy the beverage can help people like me, who tend to rush through the meditation process. If you find yourself getting sloppy with your trance meditation when attempting crystal ball reading, try tea leaf reading for a while instead. Once you have gotten the technique of tea leaf reading down, you can easily transfer those skills to the crystal ball.

Unlike crystal ball reading, which only requires the ball itself and good lighting, tea leaf reading requires a few more special supplies. First, of course, you'll a teacup and saucer. Choose a teacup that has a rounded bottom inside the cup. You will also need loose-leaf tea for the reading itself. In general, the smaller the tea leaves, the better. If you get the sort of tea that unfolds into great big leaves, you'll be left with a swampy forest covering the bottom of your cup and won't be able to distinguish any shapes. The steps to performing a tea leaf reading are as follows.

1. Ground yourself.

2. Add about three pinches of loose-leaf tea directly to the cup without a strainer and pour your hot water

over it. The most difficult part of tea leaf reading is drinking the tea without accidentally eating the leaves. This is because the tea leaves are best left to float freely in the cup as you drink. If you get addicted to tea leaf reading, I highly recommend acquiring a bombilla, a metal straw used to drink yerba mate, because it has holes in one end to strain the tea as you drink without confining the leaves. However, you don't need any specialized equipment if you sip carefully.

3. Now comes the fun part. As your tea slowly cools, you will sip and think about what questions you would like the tea leaves to answer. Tea leaf readings are a good way to relax into the process and work on entering a light trance. Sip your tea and meditate on your questions until there is as little water left in the cup as possible. It is okay if there is some water left with your leaves, but there should not be so much as to overflow your saucer when you will overturn your cup upon it.

4. This maneuver takes practice to master: Swirl the remaining water and leaves around in your cup clockwise three times and then quickly overturn the cup on a saucer.

5. Slowly lift the cup back upright and gaze into it, where the leaves should have painted themselves all around the cup. Turn the cup as much as you like in order to identify any shapes that you see. Set the cup down and sketch the contents of the cup in your sketch book, labeling any of the shapes that

you identify for later interpretation. Traditionally, the leaves in the very bottom of the cup represent the past or present, and the leaves closer to the rim represent the future and possibly destiny.

Scrying mirror

A scrying mirror is usually a darkened mirror used only for gazing and scrying. Using a scrying mirror is a very different experience from crystal ball or tea leaf reading because there are no objects you will perceive as shapes for symbolic interpretation. Instead, a scrying mirror is meant to be a backdrop for your mind to see images, as in dreams or trance meditation with closed eyes. The good news is that images seen in a scrying mirror will be more crisp and defined, and are often likened to appearing on a television set. The bad news is that a scrying mirror is a little tougher for a beginner to use because it can require a deeper trance state to trigger visions.

Scrying mirrors can be purchased, or you can make your own. My very favorite kind of scrying mirror is made with concave glass, like the sort that you might buy at a clock shop to put on the face of a clock, but then overturned so that it is like a bowl. The bowl shape of the concave scrying mirror will create an optical illusion that flips your mirror image and makes the light of your image appear to float, which in turn can inspire your mind to see more three-dimensional images.

A simpler, cheaper, and easier scrying mirror can be made out of a picture frame. Choose a picture frame without too many embellishments around the edges, as decorations will draw your eye away from the center of the scrying mirror, where you really want to see the action. A circular or oval frame is the best, because your eyes actually track to the corners of a square or rectangular frame as well. Frame a piece of black velvet to absorb all the light. Some choose instead to paint the back of the picture frame glass with black paint or to simply use black paper as the backing.

Lighting when using a scrying mirror can be important. In contrast to bright crystal ball lighting, candlelight or dim mood lighting is entirely appropriate and helpful for using a scrying mirror. You will want to avoid having any light sources reflecting directly off of the glass and into your eye, otherwise all you will be looking at is that white speck of light. Here are the steps to follow to attempt to scry with a scrying mirror. Beforehand, decide how long your session will last.

1. Ground yourself.

2. Start quiet and clear-minded meditation.

3. Allow yourself to go into a trance through controlled breathing or dance.

4. Open your eyes and sit with your scrying mirror, gazing into the center of it. Allow your eyes to gaze in a soft focus, as if staring at an object through and beyond the mirror. Try not to let your eyes move at all. Sit in this receptive meditation for the predetermined amount of time.

5. When the time is up, record anything you saw in your sketchbook—even if it was only your own reflection.

Again, don't be disheartened if you find scrying mirror sessions difficult. If you don't see anything your first time, continue your attempts daily and try some of the troubleshooting methods in the section about trance meditation in chapter 2. It may be that you simply need to lengthen the session or reduce your grounding before using your scrying mirror. You can move on to other scrying methods listed here before you have mastered your scrying mirror, as smoke scrying and fire scrying are very different experiences. Water scrying can be more similar to using a mirror.

Smoke scrying

If you have severe asthma or a sensitivity to smells or particulates, skip this one. Smoke scrying is an ancient technique that was frequently associated with entheogens, or sacred drugs burned in many different cultures. However, smoke scrying can easily be done with your favorite incense. Some common incenses used for psychic work include cinnamon, jasmine or vanilla. My favorite to use is frankincense, because I can get frankincense resin pretty smoky without having to keep throwing dried herb into the censer, distracting me from my visioning work. You will also find that some incenses allow the smoke to rise more slowly than others, giving you more time to focus on your vision. Yes, you can use stick incense, but I like burning charcoal with my incense so I can modify the amount of smoke produced. You can make your own censer by simply filling the bottom of a metal container with sand.

Smoke scrying is similar to crystal ball reading and tea leaf reading because you will be identifying shapes in the smoke. However, smoke scrying is an entirely different experience because the smoke will be moving and changing shape as you scry. That means that the shapes can change meaning as the smoke disperses, and that many shapes can flood your perceptions during the scrying session, as you won't have time to examine one shape. You'll need some pretty good lighting for smoke scrying, because smoke can easily disappear in darkness or flickering candlelight.

1. Ground yourself.

2. Light the charcoal for your incense and add a pinch of incense.

3. (Optional) Try entering a trance before smoke scrying to see if it helps you experience visions.

4. Open your eyes, add more incense to the charcoal, and gaze at the smoke as it rises, trying to identify shapes in the smoke as it dissipates. The shapes will change rapidly, so you'll have to trust your first impressions.

5. Sketch any images you saw in the smoke, and write down any interpretations that may come to you immediately.

The challenge in smoke scrying is learning to trust what you first see, since it won't linger. Thus, smoke scrying is a memory test and is more deeply intuitive than some other forms of scrying. If you find smoke scrying more challenging, you can skip it and come back to it later. Since I am a naturally more impulsive person, I sometimes find smoke scrying more freeing because it gives me permission to work quickly through the imagery. Fire scrying, which follows, has the same benefit.

Fire scrying

Fire scrying can be more fun than smoke scrying, as well as easier to perform, because staring at fire is a good way to enter a trance. As a bonus, fire provides its own lighting, so you can use dim mood lighting or bright natural light depending on your preference. There are two common ways to perform fire scrying—with a candle, and with hot coals. Although most people have easier access to a candle than to hot coals, I highly recommend the latter practice, as it is extremely effective. Trance scrying near a fire can be dangerous, so you don't have to try to enter a deep trance. It is also best to have somebody with you, and remember to keep your distance from the fire so that if you fall over or drift off, there won't be a problem.

Fire scrying with hot coals:

1. Ground yourself.

2. Build a "need fire" by thinking about what question you'd like answered as you start the fire in a fireplace or safe fire pit.

3. Allow the fire to burn hot enough that red hot embers develop. You want the heat to be such that there is a bed of glowing and flickering light. Those flashes of light are called salamanders, and they will be the source of your visions. Use a fire poker to arrange the fire so that those coals are exposed enough to view without cooling them too much. Make sure there is a safe barrier between you and the fire.

4. Position yourself a safe distance from the fire and gaze into the bed of coals, identifying shapes from the glowing forms you see.

5. Sketch what you see as soon as you identify a shape, along with your impressions.

Fire scrying with a candle:

1. Ground yourself.

2. Light a yellow candle in a candleholder and place it in a safe spot like a fireplace or upon cement so you can gaze for a long time without worry of starting a fire or leaving burn marks.

3. Seat yourself a safe distance from the candle and gaze at the flickering flame, identifying shapes that you see, especially in the base surrounding the wick.

4. Sketch what you see as soon as you identify a shape along with any immediate interpretations that jump to mind.

Water scrying

Water scrying is a similar experience to the scrying mirror in that you won't be looking for shapes, but instead will be relying on a trance state to see clear visions. Water scrying can also be more challenging if you are used to using a concave scrying mirror; the optical illusion of the concave surface won't be there to help inspire your mind. However, those who have been using flat scrying mirrors may find water scrying easier. As with the mirror, you'll have to position your bowl of water so that lights don't reflect directly off of the surface of the water and distract your eye. Dim mood lighting or candlelight may be preferable to bright lights.

For water scrying, I use two different kinds of bowls for different experiences. One is a silver bowl full of filigree imprints, and the other is a black bowl. A black bowl is more traditional, and provides a dark background like the scrying mirror. A silver bowl brings flickers of light to your scrying, adding some of the feel of fire scrying or crystal ball reading. As a beginner, I recommend trying one of each, so you find out what is easiest. If you can only try one, I recommend the traditional dark black bowl. Fill it with water as close to the brim as you can. An optional old trick is to add some black ink to the water in order to make the surface act more mirror-like, but I usually water scry without ink. The two experiences are different and should be tried; you may be able to see clairvoyant visions below the surface as well as above more easily without the ink.

1. Ground yourself.

2. Begin quiet and clear-minded meditation.

3. Enter a trance through controlled breathing or dance.

4. While seated, relax and open your eyes to gaze into the bowl of water. Soften your focus as if you were looking at a spot beyond the bowl of water. Wait in this receptive meditation for a timed session.

5. When the time is up, sketch any images you may have seen, even if all you saw was your own

reflection. Write down any interpretations that
spring to mind at the time of your water scrying.

I'd like to suggest an extra scrying exercise for water scrying I have done with much enjoyment. Since water represents
emotions, water scrying can help you get to the emotional base
of an issue, and this exercise helps prime you for that. Pick out
a poem that is either one of your favorite and most emotional
poems, or one that you might have a bit of a difficult time
interpreting. Say a line from the poem and then gaze into the
water, bidding your senses to make sense of the poem through
your visions while water scrying. Sketch the result in your
sketchbook and then say another line and move on. I have
produced wonderful books of poetry this way, using water-
color paints to interpret some of my favorite spiritual works.

All of these scrying methods bring tools to your hands to
help you inspire your mind's eye to bring forth images right
in front of your real eyes. Many clairvoyants only work with
tools, even when they perform professional readings for clients. However, some believe that scrying tools are a crutch.
That is because they create a sort of boundary between the
viewer and the visions being seen. When things only appear
in a scrying tool—and never right in front of your eyes
during your everyday life at work, home, or school—the
world seems more safe and predictable. That isn't necessarily
a bad thing, and in fact some boundaries may be necessary
for people who might have naturally disruptive visions in
other contexts. However, it is possible to see visions without
tools, so I'd like to teach you a technique for seeing auras.

Auras

An aura is thought to be the visible representation of the life energy of the universe. Around a person, an aura looks like a halo or a cocoon of color, light, or haze. All humans have an aura, and some clairvoyants can see auras around animals, plants, and even inanimate objects. When I studied martial arts, I traveled to visit my sensei's teacher, who was excited to speak with me about auras. He said that he can see the aura of an opponent even when his back is turned. As you might imagine, that means that an aura can extend quite far away from a person's body. Auras can also stay quite close in to the body as well, and they may expand or contract due to a person's emotions, health, and intentions.

Auras can look very different on different people, and can even take the shape of other imagery, especially if the person is trying to shield him- or herself from being noticed or emotionally attacked. I'll give you an example from when I was taught to see auras for the first time. A group of friends and I were taking a class on viewing auras. The teacher told us to pair up with a partner and switch off for the various exercises.

With my first partner, the teacher told the person being viewed to imagine being on a stage and putting on an excellent performance. A large audience was noticing her and approving of her. As my subject sat and I concentrated on seeing her aura, I was surprised at how vividly it expanded from her midsection and seemed to envelop a few feet around her in all directions with a hazy yellow light.

We switched partners, and she told the next person to put up a psychic shield, a barrier to protect the aura from the world around him. She told him to imagine that somebody was trying to pick a fight with him and he was to ward that person off. When I looked at him, his aura seemed closer to his body and rigid, almost as if he were encased in a coffin. When I told him of my vision, he told me that he often visualizes himself inside an Egyptian sarcophagus.

My third partner was also told to think of protecting herself from attack. When I looked at her, it seemed as if her aura was made of spiky fur with tooth-like extensions around her face. When I described her aura, she told me that she envisions herself as an angry mama bear when she wants to feel protected, so it turned out that her aura took on aspects of that animal.

How to see auras

Before I tell you how to see an aura, I'd like to warn you about a common mistake that can cause beginners to confuse an optical illusion with an aura. If you stare at any object for a long time, you will begin to see an aura due to how the human eye works. Here is an example. Find a brightly colored object, such as a sticky note, and stare at it for a minute without moving your eyeballs at all. Then, look away from the note. You should see a residual image of the object's shape, as well as some odd coloration surrounding the shape that represents its aura. You may notice that the color you see is opposite the object color on the color wheel. So, if you were to stare at a red object, you would see a green color where the object had been.

The reason that you see residual color is because the rods and cones in your eyes get fatigued from being overstimulated by the color during your staring. If you try staring at the object again, you may see a reverse-colored haze surrounding the object. That is not its aura, but the optical illusion that results from fatigued eyes. You can avoid this trick on your eyes by keeping your eyes moving while looking for an aura, and by looking away and trying again if you notice the aura you are seeing is a contrasting color. For example, if a person wearing a bright red shirt seems to have a green aura, look away and then try again with your eyes moving along his or her outline to verify that your eyes aren't just tricking you.

Aura viewing can be tricky for some people, because beginners may need to enter a light trance while still being "with it" enough to keep eyes moving and avoid the optical illusion described above. I suggest that you try aura viewing without going into a trance at first, and then add a trance state if you are unsuccessful.

Get a another person to volunteer for your aura viewing. Beginners are most successful learning to view auras around people instead of animals or plants because our brains are trained to be interested in and sensitive to other people's emotional and energetic states. If you think of it one way, aura viewing is a visual extension of our natural interpersonal empathy. Your volunteer should be comfortable around you and not at all fearful of clairvoyance, because anxiety can cause the aura to contract and become less visible.

1. Have your human volunteer sit comfortably and close their eyes. Instruct the volunteer to imagine a situation in which they would like to be noticed—for example, when delivering an impassioned speech on a street corner or when

trying to catch the eye of an attractive person at a busy party. This energetic state will cause your volunteer's aura to expand and become more vibrant. Instruct your volunteer to hold that scenario as long as possible.

2. Sit comfortably and begin quiet and clear-minded meditation.

3. (Optional) Enter a light trance through controlled breathing.

4. Open your eyes and look first at the head of your volunteer, then at the midsection. Run your eyes all over the outline of your volunteer's form looking for visual differences in color, brightness, or focus around his or her body. You might notice that the world gets a little blurry, or that the lighting in the room seems more dim or bright around certain areas. Notice changes or differences in the aura, but try not to let your eyes linger more than a few seconds to avoid optical illusions. As you view your volunteer's aura, speak aloud about what you see so your volunteer will remember it for you. You can request that he or she take notes for you, if you wish.

How to create aura drawings

Drawings are a wonderful way to keep track of how auras can change over time, and a good way to get to know your various subjects. Unless you're planning to give the sketches away as gifts, you need not worry about your artistic skills, as the point of an aura drawing is to be able to tell the difference from one aura to the next, or to notice changes in an aura. Aura drawing will also help you slowly withdraw from using a trance state, and to keep your eyes moving to avoid optical illusions.

I like to do my aura drawings with colored pencils, because I can change the intensity of the aura by pressing harder or more lightly as I go. Paints would be more tricky, as you would have to take time to mix the correct color intensity. I like to just start out with some primary colors and focus upon shape and pressure, even if I am not getting too terribly accurate with the exact shade.

Aura drawing follows the same steps as the usual aura viewing, except that you may need to omit the trance state in order to keep your wits about you to draw. Before getting started with the aura drawing, I like to draw the outline of the actual person, animal, plant or object that I am drawing, so that I won't be wasting time drawing that while hastily sketching out an aura. Auras can shift and change, so you will have to draw a quick outline first and make note of the colors in the aura, forgoing any perfectionist details until after you have the gist of it.

As a beginner, aura drawing may take some time, so you might not want to first try it on a human volunteer. In fact, aura drawing is a great opportunity to experiment. Here are some homework assignments that you can try in order to improve your aura drawing skill.

1. Does your reflection have an aura? Try drawing a portrait of yourself using a mirror and attempt to incorporate your aura. Remember to purposely extend your aura by imagining yourself trying to be noticed.

2. Sketch the aura of your own hand.

3. If you have a pet, try to sketch your pet's aura while he or she is sleeping.

4. Try sketching the aura of a plant.

5. Can you see auras around inanimate objects? Try an object with special meaning to you, such as one you used during the psychometry exercises.

As you practice and become more speedy with your sketches, try making aura drawings of human volunteers. You can even give away some aura drawings as gifts, since they make an extra special personalized present. Drawing a person's aura takes away from the embarrassment of drawing peoples' faces or bodies accurately, since you can just make an outline if you like. I'm not the most talented artist myself, but drawing somebody's aura somehow seems to capture the essence of that person a simple sketch alone would not. I once sketched the aura of a stranger's daughter and had the mother's eyes well up with tears as she told me that the sketch looked just like her daughter. To me, the drawing looked like my usual rough attempt to try to draw a human along with an aura. However, to the mother, the appearance of her daughter's bright and cheerful aura on paper was the most accurate depiction of her beloved child that she had ever seen. If you are a good artist, you may have a career ahead of you, or at least a good idea for holiday and birthday gifts.

What auras mean

Most people are excited to learn the color of their aura, however aura colors can change frequently. Also, perception of an aura's color may depend more upon the clairvoyant seeing the aura than the person whose aura is being viewed. We'll explore more about the symbolism of colors in chapter 5. For now, you should know that it is more important to notice a dramatic change or an anomaly in an aura.

For example, if one area of the aura is darker or more contracted than another, it may be an indication of low energy or a lack of flow of energy. Those aura changes can happen right before the onset of an illness or after an injury, so they can help predict when a person may need time to heal or to go in to visit the doctor. By contrast, if an aura becomes more expansive and bright, it might be an indication that they have too much empathy, and are wearing themselves a little thin. An aura that is overflowing can be controlled by practicing some grounding.

It can be tempting to try to "fix" somebody's aura, if you notice that it is shaped differently from yours, or from the other auras you see. For example, if most people's auras conform basically to their body shape, and you see somebody with a distinctly pear shaped aura, it is natural to want to try to visualize the aura conforming to expectations. Try to refrain from purposely visualizing other peoples' auras, especially without permission. Just as everybody's bodies and fingerprints are different, auras are naturally unique. Visualization may affect and change a person's aura in a negative way, so you should practice being a passive observer of auras, rather than using active visualization techniques.

Holey Stones

A holey stone is a rock with a naturally occurring hole in it. Holey stones have been collected in many cultures and are sometimes worn on pieces of string for protection from harm. Clairvoyants can also use these stones by gazing through the hole to see visions. Finding a holey stone is said to be lucky, but you can also purchase one from a rock shop. Some clairvoyants even make their own by drilling a hole in a rock if no naturally formed holey stone is available.

The purpose of the holey stone is to train your brain to learn that whenever you look through the stone is the proper time to see clairvoyant visions. The best way to start working with your holey stone is to set aside daily time for practice. Soon you will be conditioned to the idea that visions occur only when looking through the hole. After you've grown accustomed to using your holey stone, you may simply look through it at any time to see visions instantly. In this way, a holey stone is an excellent way for the beginner clairvoyant to progress to advanced practice.

Steps for practicing with your holey stone once a day:

1. Ground yourself.

2. Begin quiet and clear-minded meditation.

3. Enter a trance by dancing or controlled breathing while holding your holey stone.

4. Open your eyes and look through the hole with your dominant eye.

5. Once you see something, sketch it in your sketchbook and write down any impressions as to its meaning.

The trick to this practice is to keep on trying every day until you can complete the entire activity successfully every time. Over time, you can phase out the trance state and then work on reducing your meditation time in order to achieve an instant grounding and a clairvoyant state whenever you gaze through your holy stone.

When seeking omens, you can also gaze through your holey stone and take everything that you view through it as an omen. This removes the potentially exhausting duty of expectantly looking for patterns and meaning throughout your day, and instead limits your omen hunting to a specific place and time. For example, look in chapter 3 in the section about omens and watching the flight of birds as the answer to a question. You can also ask for a sign to appear through your holey stone and then watch to see if anything happens. Even if an ordinary squirrel were to cross your path while looking through a holey stone, you should consider it significant. In this way, the use of the stone releases you the rest of the time from having to puzzle over the significance of each everyday occurrence.

Having Visions

If you succeeded at the aura viewing exercises, it means that you have "seen things" with your own eyes that are not always seen by everyone. In our culture, it is generally considered to be unusual or even detrimental to see things that aren't in the visible spectrum, so you might be developing some associated concerns, or perhaps it's just strange looks from your coworkers when you mention their auras. We'll go into the stigma that surrounds seeing things a little bit later in this book.

By now, some readers who have diligently practiced all the exercises may be seeing other visions more often. Perhaps a psychic flash imprints itself on your mind's eye, like a daydream that tells the truth. Or perhaps you are beginning to see other common sights of myth and legend, like flashes of fairy lights in the garden, angels in the clouds, or ghosts or shadowy creatures that stir in the night. If you ever feel like you are out of control of those visions and need them to go away, you can ground yourself quickly and tell any entities to "go away" in no uncertain terms.

Being clairvoyant isn't exactly like a switch that you can flip on and off. It is more like a leaky faucet. Nobody can turn it off completely; some people just ignore the drip, and others divert the flow. You will have to learn how to metaphorically modulate the flow of your faucet by turning the handle at will and having an appropriate bowl to catch drops so they won't cause a flood or go to waste.

How do I know I'm not crazy?

People who "see things" should be locked up in the loony bin, right? Wrong. Even if you can't always control your visions, you are *not* going crazy. The actual symptom of mental illness associated with visual hallucinations is called psychosis. Psychosis can include hallucinations of all the senses: Visual, auditory, tactile, and even smelling or tasting things that are not there. Psychosis can also include delusions or disordered thinking.

Clairvoyance is different from psychosis in several important ways. Firstly, clairvoyance presents itself as pictures in your mind's eye, as opposed to perceiving things in the room that are not there physically. If you have a passing daydream in which you vividly see a unicorn in your mind's eye so clearly that you can count the spirals on its horn and the stripes on its mane, that is not a hallucination. If you stop your car in traffic because you feel you must allow a similarly vivid unicorn to cross the road, that's a hallucination. A more detailed list of the difference between hallucinations and clairvoyant visions is included later in this book if your concern is serious.

Most importantly, clairvoyance has a valuable place in spiritual life, whereas psychosis causes significant dysfunction in one or more important parts of your life. If your clairvoyance is helpful but sometimes alarming, that's okay. But if fears of your clairvoyance keep you from leaving the house, keeping a job, or having a relationship, you might be experiencing symptoms of psychosis.

What should you do if you think you have a real problem? Visit your general physician. Don't worry, nobody can make you treat a mental illness (with drugs or hospitalization) unless you are a danger to yourself or others, or if you are severely disabled. You need to visit a regular doctor first to see if there are any other serious problems that need addressing. Hallucinations aren't just caused by mental illness; they can also be caused by serious and even deadly problems like seizure disorders, brain tumors, or organ failure, so you'll need to rule those out if you have frequent visual hallucinations that disrupt your life.

If, however, you simply find yourself needing to put some boundaries on your clairvoyance before it turns into a problem, you can do several things. My best recommendation would be to make sure that you are completely grounded before and after any clairvoyant work. You can focus on dream work and meditation with your eyes closed if it makes you feel more comfortable. Also, you can make sure to keep as much of a boundary between your clairvoyant sessions and your everyday life as possible. That means dismissing any visions from your mind by grounding yourself if they appear unbidden, and telling yourself that you'll set time aside to have a clairvoyant session later.

Another good way to set up a boundary between your everyday life and your clairvoyant sessions is to always use a tool, such as one of the scrying tools mentioned earlier. Professional clairvoyants sometimes choose to use tools exclusively. And a real clairvoyant can even limit his or her practice to divination. However, there are some people who feel like they are too limited by tools, preferring to see beautiful or interesting visions in places other than a crystal ball or another scrying medium. To these, I recommend a holey stone.

Exercises

1. Grab a few friends and meditate as a group. How does meditation in a group setting feel different? Do you feel that there is more energetic power multiplied through you, or is it just distracting?

2. Pick a divination tool to research and try.

3. Find a willing partner and take turns viewing each other's auras. The partner being viewed should try to expand his or her aura by imagining a scenario in which he or she would like being noticed. Then, the person being viewed should try contracting or shielding the aura by imagining a situation in which one needs to be guarded. Discuss the differences between the two.

4. Go on a short nature walk and keep a lookout for omens.

four

Practical Applications of Clairvoyance and Reading

O f course, there's no sense in being a clairvoyant unless you can make the skill useful in your own life and the lives of others. Otherwise, all your hard work would only result in fun stories to tell at parties. That would eventually become boring and discourage you from putting in real effort. There are three ways clairvoyance can help you, and those three ways became the motto for my fortune telling business: Discovery, confirmation, and empowerment.

discovery: Clairvoyant visions can help you discover potential future paths in life, such as what might happen if you decided between two career choices. They can also show you what really happened in past events about which you are not clear, such as those that happened before you were born or can't remember, or even reveal the truth about present events, all of which can help you make important decisions.

confirmation: Clairvoyant visions can confirm what you already know in your heart, such as the faithfulness of a lover or the rightness of a decision to end a relationship. Clairvoyant visions can also confirm the persistence of life after death, if you choose to seek visions of ghosts.

empowerment: A clairvoyant vision can also be a source of advice for how to proceed. Certainly the discoveries and confirmations can already inform your decisions, however clairvoyant messages can also convey advice about the best course of action. Who is that concerned consciousness and wisdom behind the advice you receive? Different clairvoyants have different theories, but none of us really know for sure.

What You May See When Working on Clairvoyance

When working on your clairvoyance, your ability may grow so slowly that you don't even notice it. Think about how you grew physically as a person from a tiny baby into an adult. You probably didn't notice those inches adding to your height as you grew, but year to year there was certainly a difference. Likewise, your clairvoyant ability may progress from something nearly imperceptible to a startling psychic power. For that reason, I'd like to go over what you might see when you're just starting out as a clairvoyant. You might recognize these as things that you've already seen. Otherwise, keep your eyes peeled. When you know what to expect, you won't miss those important first experiences.

Firstly, notice how ideas take on visual characteristics in your mind. For example, when sounds and words appear as a picture in your mind's eye, that's often considered to be synesthesia, a natural interconnectedness of the senses. For example, can you see music? Does the number four have a color? For me, the number four is always green. When I think of the number, I don't see the color green with my physical eyes, but in my mind I immediately think of the color green every time.

I always saw sounds visually, especially with my eyes closed. A loud pop or the beat of a drum looks like a flash of white light behind my closed eyelids. It looks so real that the imaginary light startles me just as much as the sound if I am trying to sleep when I hear a crash. It is as if my brain makes its own lightning to the thunder. One example of musical clairvoyance helped me a lot when I was a child.

As a kid, I had no idea that other people could not see sounds when they closed their eyes. I used to visit the Seattle Wind Symphony with my parents and volunteer at their booth selling snacks and CDs. One day, I had a terrible tummy ache so I went to lie down on a bench, hoping that I would feel better. I closed my eyes and I could see the music flowing out of the hall as a ribbon of color and light that was floating through the air like a scarf on the wind. I also noticed that my pain was like an angry white light gleaming in the pit of my stomach inside my body.

In my mind's eye, I could manipulate the beautiful ribbon of music, so I visualized it floating down over me and wrapping around my hurting belly. The soft colors of the musical ribbon closed around the angry white light of my pain until the cracks were sealed and I could no longer see the pain. As long as I held this picture in my mind, my pain was alleviated. To this day, I still use this clairvoyance technique to cure my pain with concentration. I have found that it works with the visual representations I see of ambient sound, not just beautiful music. I'm not saying that this technique will work for everybody, especially beginners, but I did want to include it as a practical example of how clairvoyance can affect your life directly. This also shows how clairvoyance can develop naturally from your experience of your senses.

Not everybody will experience clairvoyance as a television screen inside their heads. It is important to know that clairvoyant visions can be useful no matter the manner in which they appear.

How you see things

I can't stress enough how different individual experiences of clairvoyance may be, and as you start out as a beginner you might have your experience of clairvoyance evolve naturally. For some people, they jump right to being able to see visions of people, animals, and other things as if they were in the same room. For example, when I go to religious services, I often see clairvoyant visions right in front of my eyes that add to my experience of the service. I might see a crown of flowers appear on the head of a clergy person and then disappear just as quickly, for example.

However, some people don't start out with such startling experiences. In fact, those who are not visual people will never see a vision of a person, animal, or a clear object in front of their eyes. Some people may see a variety of different sorts of visions. Even though a person is capable of seeing clairvoyant visions right before their eyes, it doesn't mean that person can't also have more subtle visual experiences behind closed eyelids.

Though I do see interesting sights, it only happens sometimes; subtle clairvoyant moments happen all the time, however. Some visions are just an image in my mind, the same way I might visualize a character in a book. For a split second, a picture flashes across my mind. It isn't scary and dramatic, and it doesn't cause me to crumple over in awe. It doesn't feel like such thoughts are pushed into my mind by any supernatural force. In fact, it feels rather ordinary, like a flight of fancy of my own imagination. Just as dreams while you are asleep can be clairvoyant visions, daydreams while you are awake can be clairvoyant visions too.

One common example is "seeing" somebody's face flash across your mental landscape right before the telephone rings with that person on the other line. So far, I have bought two houses, and I had visions of each of them before I ever saw them in real life. Again, these visions were just like ordinary daydreams in which I populated my mind with the idea of the house I wanted, complete with details like rose bushes outside. In the case of my most recent house purchase, when I went to tour a house with my realtor, I was startled at how familiar it looked to my vision. It served as an emotional confirmation for me that the house was the right one on which to place a bid.

How things appear

In a clairvoyant vision, things may appear very similar to your real life visions or they may be somewhat different. For me, clairvoyant visions can span this range depending on what techniques that I am using. For example, people in my clairvoyant visions might seem like people that I see in dreams, a collage of different characteristics of people that I know. For example, I had a clairvoyant vision when meditating about starting up a new community group. I saw the place where I would hold the meetings in my vision, but the people who were present seemed vague and difficult to place. It was as if physical features of the people at the meeting were just a combination of features of people I already knew.

From that vision, I understood that my brain was trying to fill in the blanks by showing me that I would build a community made up of friends. The important point wasn't to identify the individuals involved, but rather to give me the impetus that it was the right thing to do. Sure enough, after I organized my community group, I immediately made friends with the people involved, even if they were strangers or mere acquaintances before.

Your clairvoyant visions may vary in other ways too. As a beginner, when you try clairvoyance with your eyes open you might have startling success right away. Some of the people and things I see in visions are no different from seeing real people and objects in the same room as myself, but it is in a fleeting and spiritual context. For others, clairvoyant visions may be invisible to your physical eyes while still seeming to appear in front of them. I know that sounds weird, so let me give you another example you can use.

If you're sitting some place that has a doorway, look at the doorway and imagine a jolly six-foot man standing in the doorway. Even though you're not seeing this imaginary man, you can probably tell with your eyes whether he has to stoop down to not hit the top of the doorway. You can probably tell about where his shoulders would be just by eyeballing the door. You can even guess whether he can raise his hands to touch the ceiling. Even though you aren't seeing the man with your eyes, you can still get a lot of information from your brain that is highly visual in nature.

My own clairvoyance has developed and changed over the years. I used to see auras in the same way I described earlier. I wouldn't see a literal color around the person, but I could know and understand things about the aura just like the imaginary man in the doorway. By looking at a person, I would have a sense of how far the aura extended around him or her as well as the aura's color. Now I do see more literal visions of auras exclusively. Part of that may be due to the uniqueness of my own brain, but I also believe that some of it has to do with my careful development of useful clairvoyant skills. Even if you're very new to clairvoyance and feeling like you're "faking it" by using your visualization techniques, have faith that you are developing real skills.

Not all clairvoyant visions are subtle, even with eyes closed. I often use clairvoyant visions in meditation to speak spiritually with the divine. When meeting with deities in my mind, they often look larger than life and more vivid. The color of skin or hair of a divine person in my mind may be surreal and more intense than could ever be seen in life. It is almost as if my brain is registering colors that are off the visible spectrum at times. There is no way that I can mistake some of those visions for ordinary daydreams, because they cause an emotional part of me to sit up and take notice. It is the beauty of such a vision that is remarkable.

In such clairvoyant visions I can pray out loud or in my head and converse with divinity. Clairvoyance is an amazing tool for spirituality. It is one thing to talk to God without clairvoyance, but quite another to look the divine in the face as if you were having tea together. Of all the forms of clairvoyance I write about in this book, the simple technique of meditating and praying while allowing divine visions to appear is the one I use most frequently.

What You May Experience When Working on Clairvoyance

As you work on your clairvoyance, you'll find that you start developing visual skills in many areas of your life. You might even become more of a visual learner, which can help you in future studies of any subject. You'll also be developing that psychic side of yourself, so you may find yourself using clairvoyance inadvertently. Your newfound reliance on psychic abilities might surprise you, too. You don't have to be scared; it isn't as if visions are going to pop up unannounced all the time. Rather, you'll start using clairvoyance as a natural extension of your senses.

Remember that common example of picturing a person's face right before the phone rings? Well, now imagine that as you get more practice as a clairvoyant, you start seeing the person as they call every time your phone rings. That's the sort of progression I am talking about. I tend to have another version of that clairvoyant vision, in that the faces of people I need to call pop into my head right at the moment when they need to talk to me the most. In that way, I tend to be the first person to learn important news from friends and family, be it good or bad.

When you go about your day, you might start taking in additional clairvoyant information about the people and places in your life. When you enter a new room you've never visited before, you might have pictures fly into your mind like daydreams gone wild. They will be easily dismissed, of course, but pay attention to them and jot down some notes if you get a chance. You may find that it is the clairvoyant part of your mind trying to send you a message. When you shake hands with a new person, you also might gain some clairvoyant information such as seeing an aura, or having a symbolic image flash across your mind. It isn't wrong to use your clairvoyant sense when interacting with people, even if they don't know that's what you're doing. Clairvoyance is a natural part of you, and should be accepted as part of your full potential as a human being.

Clairvoyance also has the awesome side effect of anticipating seeing clairvoyant visions. I dreamed and even meditated before I started working on my clairvoyant ability, but now I find it hard to "waste" a night's sleep or meditation session without thinking about a question I want answered by clairvoyance. Every time when I lie down to sleep and many of the times I sit down to meditate, I automatically first decide what topics I might want to have in a vision. If I have problems, I try to work them out in a visual way while I sleep or rest. In fact, I have to force myself to go back to the ways of meditation by emptying my mind of everything including clairvoyant visions. I do make the effort, though, because I believe that the ability to clear your mind is helpful and vital to a clairvoyant.

Expect your interest in clairvoyance to wax and wane as with anything else in life. If your visions are subtle, you might find yourself pushing harder to try to find some success or slacking off when feeling discouraged. Conversely, if you have strong clairvoyant visions, you may find yourself becoming briefly obsessed with clairvoyant tips and tricks and then suddenly bored. These are all natural phases of learning something new. Cut yourself some slack and commit to a reasonable schedule of learning. A few minutes every day can keep your skills from fading and allow you to learn new things without feeling overwhelmed or bored.

Seeing Something for the First Time

It might feel a little intimidating and exciting if you are still preparing for some of your first clairvoyant visions. Remember that even if you're experienced with some types of clairvoyant visions, you may have different experiences ahead of you as you work hard on developing your ability. If you don't know what to expect, you are in for an interesting and fascinating ride.

Above all, remember that clairvoyance is normal, and that the exercises in this book are designed to bring about the experiences in a gentle progression. So, you don't have to worry about crossing a point of no return with your clairvoyant work. If you decide to change your mind about any exercise before you see a clairvoyant vision, you can simply ground all of the energy and quit.

Don't allow yourself to get flustered. As a teenager, I was particularly excitable. Whenever I would see a vision of a ghost, it would make me jumpy for weeks. It felt like there was another ghost sighting around every corner, and I would get quite spooked and silly about the entire experience. Your emotional state can color the way you experience clairvoyant visions, so work at keeping your clairvoyant sessions light and fun.

You can use your excitement to your advantage, too. Don't forget to pat yourself on the back anytime you do see something that could be a clairvoyant vision. Even small successes can be a reason to celebrate. When you reward yourself for working hard and achieving the results you want, you train your brain to keep doing what you want and possibly to increase your clairvoyant potential.

However, if you are eagerly awaiting your first clairvoyant vision, you'll have to expect subtlety. As your skills build on top of your previous experiences and talents, a beginner may notice clairvoyant visions that only differ only very slightly from what you have been dealing with before. Daydreams that seem strangely more compelling are easy to brush aside and forget. After all, we've been spending our whole lives training our brains to ignore extraneous information, and now you're working on fine-tuning new observational skills.

Your first clairvoyant vision may be an especially vivid dream or daydream. Very much like what you've experienced before without even trying, but with something that catches your attention. There's something about clairvoyant visions that can make them feel a bit different than anything ordinary. However, that "something" can be hard to notice for the beginner just developing his or her clairvoyant powers. It could be a pattern, emotional feeling, or something especially beautiful or unusual. It is the part that catches your attention, not the vision itself, that you'll have to train yourself to notice at first when your clairvoyant visions seem painfully ordinary.

For example, I have a friend who only seems to have clairvoyant dreams or daydreams after she sees a series of numbers on the clock. So, if the clock reads 2:22 pm, and she then has a daydream about a road trip, she'll pay special attention to that vision. Was she driving a new car or an old car? What season was outside the window? What do cars and roads mean to her symbolically? Ordinarily, you wouldn't pick apart every single fleeting daydream, because that would be exhausting and take up your entire life. But the pattern of numbers alerts my friend that this is her brain trying to tell her about an incoming clairvoyant vision. If, right before falling asleep, the clock read 11:11 pm, you can bet she would make sure to have her dream journal ready.

Perhaps you have had moments in your life that seem especially significant as well. After a death in my family, everything seemed particularly poignant to me. When simply sitting out on my porch having a cup of tea, an emotional pall would come over me, and it would cause me to tune into my senses and become more aware. Staring into the branches of the trees, they seemed to form images of people in my life. Seeing what I did caused me to take action to reach out to those people in case they too were suffering losses. This example is simple and gentle, and it represents the sort of clairvoyant visions you might have at first, those which seem born out of emotion. Remember that just because emotion is involved in your clairvoyant visions, it doesn't make them any less valid. In fact, emotion can make them even more important.

Procedures and Tips for Performing Clairvoyant Psychic Readings

We've already gone over the procedures that are absolutely necessary for performing clairvoyant readings. At the bare minimum you should practice grounding, meditation, and recording your observations. We've also gone over some optional skills to develop, such as trance work and divination. Here are some more exercises you can add to your clairvoyant reading repertoire. You may find they improve your accuracy and precision.

Prayer before reading

Saying a prayer before performing a clairvoyant reading is a good practice to establish intention for those who believe in any sort of deity or deities. It can even be a good tool for agnostics to get in touch with the higher self or to establish a predictable practice for alerting your subconscious to start working and churning out visions. Typically as clairvoyants, we are concerned with three things when doing a clairvoyant reading: We want our readings to be correct and precise, we want our readings to be helpful and successful in the moment rather than too-little-too-late, and we want our readings to be safe and to avoid harm to ourselves or others.

If prayer is new to you, or if you're pretty rusty at prayer and coming back to it after a long absence, I'd like to offer a little assistance. Whenever I pray, I like to include several important elements, and I've developed a mnemonic using the letters in the word "PRAYING." The letters stand for the steps in the prayer process: Person listening is addressed, Raise praise, Ask for help, Your deadline is specified, Imperatives for safety are expressed, Note of thanks, and Gracious attention is given.

PERSON LISTENING
Hail, [god(s)/goddess(es)/Spirit/
Universe/higher self/etc.]

RAISE PRAISE
*You who is/are [list three positive
attributes], I praise you!*

ASK FOR HELP
*Thank you for an accurate and
precise clairvoyant reading.*

YOUR DEADLINE
NOW

IMPERATIVES FOR SAFETY
*With harm to none, and for the
highest good of all. So may it be.*

NOTE OF THANKS
*In return, I offer you [gratitude/
love and devotion/other offering].*

GRACIOUS ATTENTION
Blessed be.

*(Pause, take three deep breaths, and be silent
and alert for a clairvoyant response.)*

Precognition

Most clairvoyants or people who are enlisting in the aid of clairvoyants are interested in knowing the future. The ability to have knowledge of future events is called precognition, and it has been mentioned earlier in this book with regards to precognitive dreams. Just like in dreams, precognitive clairvoyant visions can be either literal or symbolic. In chapter 5, I'll cover some issues surrounding knowledge of the future in more depth, but for now we'll get into a little bit of theory so you'll know how to practically apply precognitive visions when reading for yourself or others.

The first and most important thing you should know is that your clairvoyant visions are not always precognitive. There are many reasons a vision you see may not come to pass. Here are the most common:

The vision was misinterpreted. Though it seemed to be literal, it turned out to be symbolic. For example, a vision of a person becoming pregnant turned out to represent a creative idea or a work project rather than a literal baby.

Actions were taken that changed the potential future you saw. The future is written in sand, not stone, and every choice you make affects your future. I like to think of the future as a framework similar to our road system. You can't really go outside the roads, those are your destiny. However, you can make turns at specific points in your life that change where you might end up. The point of a clairvoyant reading is not to see your ultimate outcome, but to see the potential places where the roads end up as well as the turning points, so that you can navigate to where you want.

You were just plain wrong. Hey, we're human and we all make mistakes. Sometimes I spill my cup of tea, forget a word on the tip of my tongue, or completely misconstrue what somebody else is saying. When you find yourself being way off base, check yourself. Are you overly tired? Hungry? Are your fears about the future causing you to imagine the worst-case scenario rather than see the truth? Are your hopes about the future causing you to blindly wish for something to happen rather than see the truth? Take a break and then try again.

The best thing that you can do to make your precognitive clairvoyance more useful is to ask the right questions. That means you'll have to think about the future as a framework of choices, not the ending of a movie (so quit asking about the ending of the movie). Otherwise you'll get confusing and contradictory outcomes without telling you anything about the turning points. Instead, before you get started on your clairvoyant session, write down your question. Start by thinking about what outcome you would like to have from the matter. If you don't know what you want, ask for the clarity to see what the best outcome might be for all concerned.

I'll give you some specific examples to transform some common questions once we get into topical readings in chapter 5.

What Is the Source Behind Clairvoyant Power and Advice?

Some people believe that all information in the universe is there for the understanding, but that most of us just don't take the time to look at it. For example, some believe that everything that has ever happened or ever will happen is stored in a place on the astral plane called the Akashic Library. Finding out your future spouse or the way you will die would be as easy as going to the library and looking at a book on the shelf.

Many believe in the existence of a higher power such as deity or spirit, our higher self, goddesses or gods who love us and wish the best for us in life. For such theistic clairvoyants, visions are messages sent by deity in the form of pictures. It is the duty of the clairvoyant to ask questions, thank the deity for answers and to carefully figure out riddles that may be contained in clairvoyant visions.

Another source of clairvoyant information can be the spirits of those who have passed, whether we knew them personally or not. Spirits can include ancestors, beloved dead friends or relatives, or simply spirits who spend time in the same places we work, live, and play. Such spirits should also be treated with respect, and it is possible to form lifelong friendships as spirit guides.

Seeing Ghosts

I was a clairvoyant in a haunted mansion, so I wasn't surprised to see ghosts. What did surprise me, however, was that there were so many of them. They looked to me like ordinary people, many of them elderly, who were wearing clothes from some other era as they shuffled about, in a mostly gloomy fashion. It didn't make sense to me because the mansion was the family home of Ezra Meeker, and was now a museum dedicated to his family.

The Meeker Mansion owners had invited clairvoyants to come hold a psychic fair on location, and they eagerly showed us around, indicating where the Meeker children had played and where their parents had spent their time. Unable to hold back my questions any longer, I blurted out, "Well why then are there old people?" Several other clairvoyants blinked at me, possibly thankful I had asked out loud the question they were all wondering.

The unruffled tour guide explained that long after Ezra Meeker had passed on, the mansion had been turned into a nursing home for the elderly. Many of them had lived out the rest of their lives, and thus died in the mansion. I shook my head and took another look around at the ghosts surrounding me. It all made sense, but it seemed so strange that the mansion was dedicated to a snapshot in time before they had ever lived or died in the place. It reminded me that we're always surrounded by ghosts ancient and contemporary.

Seeing ghosts is so important to clairvoyance that I believe it warrants its own section. In fact, some clairvoyants limit themselves (intentionally or not), to only seeing visions of ghosts rather than images of the past or future or of symbols. Some first clairvoyant experiences are ghost sightings, which can be disturbing and scary for those who never intended to look for ghosts in the first place. I'd like to explore all aspects of ghostly interactions here, so that you know what to look for and what to do when developing your clairvoyance when ghosts are in the picture.

What is a ghost?

For the purposes of this book, a ghost is the collective energetic remains of a human who once lived. There are many theories about why ghosts might remain on earth rather than dissipating or going to some sort of afterlife. Some believe ghosts remain when a human dies in the wrong way. For example, a suicide or a violent murder may cause an energetic signature to remain when that energy does not fully escape at the time of death. Another theory is that ghosts choose to remain here because of some sort of unfinished business, such as a message to impart or the need to fulfill the role of an ancestor giving help to a relative.

Ghosts may not be able to control who sees them, so it may be a case of being in the right place at the right time. I happen to believe that ghosts are very common occurrences, so it is quite likely that a clairvoyant will meet one in the wide panoply of supernatural fauna that is out there. A ghost may request assistance, such as imparting a message or escaping to an afterlife. It is up to you how much you want to interact with a ghost or help one that appears to be in need. When we reach the section on ethics in chapter 5, we'll explore a little bit more about that. For now, we'll take a look at what those interactions might look like.

What does a ghost look like to a clairvoyant?

To me, most ghosts look almost indistinguishable from normal living people. The only way I can tell them apart is if they inform me that they are ghosts, if I summon their appearance as ghosts specifically, or if there is something anomalous about the way that they dress or act. Other clairvoyants, however, may see ghosts in many different ways, as evidenced by the many descriptions of ghosts across time and cultures.

Ghosts may appear as skeletons, as translucent human forms, rotting or injured bodies, white blobs, orbs of light, or as mists. Some ghosts appear to me to even be a shifting amalgam of human features. The appearance of a ghost may seem frightening in and of itself because it may draw attention to the mortality of flesh and bone. You may have already seen a ghost before, so take note of the way that ghost appeared in your mind, because it will tend to preserve that appearance for you.

Often it isn't the appearance that lets you know whether it is a pleasant or angry spirit; even a happy skeleton looks scary. Pay attention to other clues, such as what emotions or messages you sense are coming from the spirit. Look at the body language of the spirit as if it were a living person. A spirit that makes itself larger and moves quickly with its gestures may not be as friendly as one that moves slowly with arms open to appeal to your sense of welcoming.

Are ghosts dangerous?

It is believed that some ghosts can be dangerous. In rare cases, poltergeists can move objects in a way that can be frightening or hazardous. However, paranormal events that turn into dangerous encounters are very rare indeed. Think about it:

If everyone who has ever lived and died had the potential to become a ghost, and if dangerous ghosts existed, then hearing about deaths or injuries from flying knives would be very common.

No, the more common danger of ghosts is emotional. Seeing ghosts can bring your own mortality into sharp focus. Or the ghost might say something to you that doesn't mesh with your personal spiritual beliefs, causing a personal spiritual conundrum. Ghosts can also lie, so if you're using a ghost to relay messages about the past, present, or future, you might find yourself the recipient of incorrect information. That said, there's no need to be unduly frightened of seeing spirits. Here is a simple prayer based on the format already given that can ensure spiritual protection from such encounters:

PERSON LISTENING
Hail, [god(s)/goddess(es)/Spirit/
Universe/Higher Self/etc.]

RAISE PRAISE
*You who is/are [list three
positive attributes], I praise you!*

ASK FOR HELP
*Only positive and peaceful spirits are
welcome; all negative spirits must leave.*

YOUR DEADLINE
NOW

IMPERATIVES FOR SAFETY
With harm to none, and for the
highest good of all. So may it be.

NOTE OF THANKS
In return, I offer you [gratitude/
love and devotion/other offering].

GRACIOUS ATTENTION
Blessed be.

(Pause, take three deep breaths, and be silent
and alert for a clairvoyant response.)

What if I don't want to see ghosts?

If you naturally start to see ghosts during your clairvoyant exercises, you can tell them out loud to go away. A strong command like that will work on many creatures on the astral plane, since it draws on your internal energetic power. It can also serve as a call to action to your own brain, to stop doing what it is doing so you can end your clairvoyant exercise quickly and smoothly. After giving the order (silently or aloud), ground yourself completely. The act of grounding yourself may cause all clairvoyant visions to flee from your mind, allowing you to resume your normal day.

If seeing ghosts is a regular problem for you, however, return to the clairvoyant exercises given earlier where you limit your clairvoyance to specific times and places. If you stop your clairvoyant work any time you see a ghost outside of a holey stone or crystal ball, for example, you will slowly train your brain to only interact with ghosts in those contexts, leaving the rest of your days and nights relatively specter-free.

Why do some people want to see ghosts?

If ghosts can lie and on rare occasion throw stuff, why on earth would any clairvoyant want to work with them in the first place? Some clairvoyants begin to see ghosts and simply don't want to wish them away, instead preferring to seek meaning behind the appearances of ghosts in their lives. Other clairvoyants may purposefully look for ghosts out of a morbid sense of curiosity about life after death. Most clairvoyants miss someone who has died and hope to see them again in some form. I usually love to see ghosts, and so much the better if they are ghosts of people that I have known and loved.

Since ghosts are abundant in the world and most of them are harmless, it is okay if you don't feel that you need to close yourself off from them. There is nothing wrong with exploring ghosts as a symbolic or literal part of your belief system. Regardless, training yourself how not to see them is a good practice too. Besides, ghosts can be terribly rude, and might show themselves at inopportune or private moments, so you'll want to keep yourself firmly in control of your clairvoyant sight at all times.

What if I want to see ghosts?

Traditionally, those who have wanted to see ghosts have used tools like Ouija boards or spirit boards, which feature printed letters through which a ghost can spell out messages. However, as I pointed out, ghosts are actually quite common. To see ghosts, generally one does not need to summon them, as they are already around us. If you want to make seeing ghosts a special priority, however, you might want to go through the following exercises with ghosts in mind until you can see them.

1. Call ghosts into your lucid dreams by asking to see them as you fall asleep.

2. Ask to see ghosts before you enter trance meditation.

3. Choose a form of scrying most comfortable to you, and ask to see ghosts in your scrying tool.

4. Ask to see ghosts when working with a holey stone.

By the time you progress through the exercises again with a focus exclusively on ghosts, you will be bringing them out of your subconscious and right in front of your eyes for your clairvoyant sight exercises. After you've gone through all the steps, you can pick whatever way you prefer to work with ghosts. You might stop at lucid dreaming or stick with a holey stone after you've seen your first ghost through one avenue or another.

After becoming comfortable seeing ghosts around you all the time, you might want to try summoning a specific ghost, such as that of a deceased loved one. Pick your favorite way of seeing ghosts from the steps above, and ask to see your specific ghost of choice. That ghost may or may not choose to show up for you, so if it does not appear, don't blame your clairvoyant abilities. It may be that your deceased loved one has better things to do in the afterlife than to appear as a ghost, or it may mean that the ghost simply doesn't want to talk to you right now for whatever reason. Some ghosts don't want to interfere with their loved ones' lives because they don't want to interfere with the grieving process or with somebody's ability to move on.

If, however, you are able to get a hold of a ghost you want, chances are you will want to share the messages you've received with other mutual friends or relatives. Group clairvoyant sessions with ghosts are often called séances, which will be covered in chapter 5.

Now that you are able to practice clairvoyance, you may begin to wonder about some of the basic theory behind it. As a beginner, your skills may advance in directions you don't necessarily expect, and you may struggle to find the meaning and purpose behind what you see. In this chapter, we'll confront the feelings and confusion that may come about as a result of your budding clairvoyant ability.

Interpretation

Interpretation of clairvoyant visions can often be frustrating and confusing. Rather than simply seeing the past, present, or future as if it were flashing before your eyes on a television screen, you might see symbolic representations that seem like riddles. Why might that be? Psychologist Carl Jung believed that our subconscious mind uses symbols in the form of pictures in order to process ideas. It may be that the clairvoyant part of our brains is mostly located within our subconscious. As a result, longer messages and ideas are communicated through imagery as opposed to presenting us with words, the way our conscious world does.

Symbols

A symbol, for the purposes of clairvoyant visions, is any visual image that represents an idea or concept. For example, letters are symbols because they make up sounds and words that we know. Likewise, numbers are symbols for quantities, but they also can have a deeper conceptual and spiritual meaning. Colors can symbolically represent feelings. You can see why it is important to write down the symbols as you see them, as well as your initial impressions as to what they might mean.

Jung believed that symbols in the subconscious were an important part of the human experience, and that they could sometimes be attributed to the collective subconscious of all mankind. For example, a mother Goddess might arise independently and spontaneously in many cultures, with a pregnant woman being a symbol for both fertility and abundance. Visual pictures in our minds, the type that come about through clairvoyance, are thought to originate from the subconscious and operate through the left half of the brain, the seat of artistic creativity and some aspects of spirituality. There are complicating factors to interpreting symbols, however. It would be nice if all symbolic pictures could be read as if they were universal hieroglyphs, but every person is different. Life experiences can make some symbols mean different things to different people.

My quintessential example is the symbolic representation of a bat. In Chinese culture, bats are good luck and represent happiness. In Navajo culture, bats do not have extremely positive or negative connotations but are simply messengers. In European culture, however, bats are bad luck and symbols of death. The way that seeing a bat should be interpreted depends on the individual. I happen to love bats, so if I should see one in a clairvoyant vision, I take it as a very good sign. However, if another clairvoyant is fearful of or disgusted by bats, they would likely be taken as a message of caution.

Interpretation exercise: explain it to an alien

I learned this useful exercise when I had a vision I was trying to interpret with a clairvoyant friend of mine. I was meditating on a social situation with some friends. In my vision, I saw all the friends involved (along with myself) on a giant rocking horse. The horse was rocking back and forth and I was looking confused sitting on the back of it. All of my friends were reacting in different ways. Some of my friends were shouting with joy as if the rocking horse were the most exciting experience in their lives. Some of my friends were freaking out and screaming as if they were on the back of a bucking bronco. I asked my clairvoyant friend if she could help me interpret my vision.

"What is a rocking horse?" my friend asked. I looked at her blankly. It would be very strange if she had never heard of a rocking horse. She tried again. "I am an alien," she said. "What is a rocking horse?" Smiling, I realized the game she was playing. I had to explain what a rocking horse was by breaking it down into its most basic meaning so that somebody who may have never heard of such a thing would understand. In doing so, I would be able to make sense of my vision.

I ended up explaining and describing the rocking horse thusly to my friend: "A rocking horse is a toy. It is made of wood. It moves back and forth in place with a rider on top." Suddenly, a seemingly obscure symbol had now acquired some very basic and universal features that could be applied to my social situation. The fact that it was a toy assured me that my situation wasn't a big deal. The rocking back and forth seemed to tell me that though my current situation would jostle me a little bit, it certainly wouldn't completely uproot me emotionally or socially. The wooden nature of the rocking horse suggested familiarity and the natural order of things. All in all, the image was calming, even though some of my friends in the vision were overreacting. Sure enough, as I moved forward, this symbolism fit my situation well.

Making your own symbol dictionary

The only way to make accurate sense of the symbols you see is to create your own personal symbol dictionary. Books like this one will give examples of symbolic interpretations, and many of them may match your own personal symbols. The human experience being what it is, all people on this planet share a lot in common. However, while building your own symbol dictionary you won't just be recording and memorizing what they mean. You will begin to learn the error of taking the classical interpretations at face value—oftentimes your brain may work differently.

For your symbol dictionary, I suggest acquiring a three-ring binder filled with lined paper. That way, you can write one symbol per page, move them around to insert more pages, and keep them in alphabetical order (or whatever order works for you) for quick reference. Now you can check out both your dream journal and your clairvoyant log to get inspiration for symbol dictionary. Circle all the important nouns you find, and start a page for each one. Write down the date next to your impressions about the word and what it means to you. As you go through life, experiences may change your interpretation of a symbol over time, so you can add more dated entries for each word as your understanding grows.

For example, I used to interpret the riddle of a picture of a sword between two dragons as a separation of two people. Initially, it looked like a barrier between two entities, so I made that assumption. As I continued to do clairvoyant readings for people, however, I noticed that whenever that scene turned up in the reading, the person for whom I was reading had recently suffered a car accident, either major or just a minor fender bender. My interpretation of that scene changed, and afterwards I could surprise people with the knowledge of a car accident, or even warn them about potential danger on the road in the near future.

A final word of advice about interpretation: Look at all of the symbols together in your vision and think about how their meanings interact, rather than interpreting them all in a row. After all, letters come together to form entire words, and symbolic pictures have a similar connectivity. For example, an image of a boat on the water doesn't simply mean whatever a boat means (for example, sharing) plus whatever the water means (for example, emotions), but the combination of those two. So, an interpretation would be that there will be a sharing of emotions, rather than that your life will include both the aspects of sharing and also emotional things. Telling the story of the symbols is a skill that is developed with practice, so you'll have to keep trying to put the pieces of the puzzle together until they make sense to you.

A list of what some visual symbols mean to me
Numbers

1. The individual; aggressiveness or assertiveness; birth, new beginnings, and fresh starts—or their potential

2. The tension of a new door opening; a meeting of minds; balance; union between two people; choosing between two paths

3. A new addition to a family; imbalance necessary while growth occurs; a meeting of old friends; communication that may be heartbreaking

4. Stability; secrets; the earth; the home; potential for things to come crashing down due to bad luck or poor money management

5. Hyperactivity; destruction; instability; fights or struggles; games

6. Learning; progress, moving upward through ranks; communication; receiving more blessings; increased responsibility

7. Mystery; spirituality; radical change; new perspectives; removal of obstacles

8. Power; success, hard work, prosperity; security and safety; moving forward or moving past blockages

9. Breakthroughs; happiness, good luck; rebirth; endings; stress, becoming overwhelmed; extremes; completion

Colors

red: Passion; masculine energy; fire; anger; war, danger; stopping; South; summertime

pink: Gentle love; feminine energy; friendship, caring; motherhood, young children; springtime

orange: Energy; success; masculinity; the sun; progress

yellow: Intuition; intellect and careful study; early mornings; springtime; East

green: North; fertility; money; wintertime; earth

blue: Healing; grief; West; water; strong emotions of any kind; dreams; madness

purple: Spirit; royalty; peace; feminine energy; creativity; wealth

gold: Riches; divine masculine; sunshine; summer

silver: Divine feminine; the moon; magic

black: Protection; night; a period of waiting or mourning

white: Health; new beginnings; purity and cleanliness of thought; spirituality

Example Symbols with Interpretations

airplane: Travel to distant lands; escaping the ordinary; transcending difficulty

alligator: A secret asset that may also be a dangerous one; a need for caution even if one may be in a position of power in a situation

anchor: Stagnation, lack of forward movement; security; connection with somebody or with material things that may be unhelpful

apple: Learning, teaching; health; the divine feminine

arrow: Arrows direct your attention to other things. If no other symbols are seen, an arrow pointing left can represent the past, the right represents the future. Pointing up represents progress and growth; pointing down can represent simplification or destruction

ax: A need for a sacrifice or for a process to be cut short before it becomes unproductive

baby carriage: A new baby is coming

bat: Messages from spirits; communication from a person who has recently died

bear: Protection; overwhelming emotions; base instincts

bell: A call to action; wedding bells that will soon be ringing

bird: Communication; a symbol for air travel; a messenger or watcher; a herald of a season. As mentioned earlier, specific birds traveling to the left or the right may have additional meaning, e.g., right to left movement meaning "yes" or affirmation

boat: Necessary communication about emotions. The state of the water can represent the emotions; a capsizing boat can represent being overwhelmed

book: Study and learning; the occult; intellect and ideas that will be lasting and need passing on *bottle:* Substance abuse; communication, as in a message in a bottle; intangible assets

bridge: A temporary opportunity for progress which can be missed. The bridge's state may indicate the risk associated with the chance, as well as whether the action can be taken back later on if needed

broom: A sweeping away of negativity; a couple jumping over it can mean marriage; a falling broom can mean company is coming

bull: The zodiac sign Taurus; rage; stubbornness

butterfly: Transformation; springtime; beauty; gentleness

car: Can represent a real car—be sure to describe it when performing a clairvoyant reading for another person; can also represent travel over land. The type may represent a personality

cat: Magic, witchcraft; femininity; power; hunting

chair: The necessity of waiting; a position of power; stability

chameleon: Change; trickery; going with the flow; danger avoidance

circle: Protection, boundaries; cycles of things that keep happening over and over again

cloak: Hiding from judgment or the truth; protection from discovery *clothes:* Often representing somebody's role in life, observe the clothes carefully and how they appear for clues about the individual's personality, occupation, and satisfaction with their place in the world

club: Immaturity; emotional deception; forceful sexual energy, fiery chemistry; creativity; life

coin: Prosperity, material wealth; physicality

comb: Not being able to see the forest for the trees, getting caught up in unimportant details that take the focus away from the big picture

cornucopia: Abundance; fertility; material wealth

crab: Femininity; a need for comfort; the zodiac sign Cancer

cross: Christianity; protection; a crossroads in life that will cause significant change

crown: High status; a need for attention; leadership; new roles

cup: Emotions; West; watery locations; love potential or loss if the cup is overturned

death: The ending of a relationship, project, life or things as you know it

deer: A masculine symbol—antlers represent the emotional or physical maturity of the man concerned depending on size and appearance

devil or demon: Negativity, especially one's own negativity that can lead to a downfall

diamond: Material wealth, physical success; friendship; earth *dinosaur:* The distant past; something that has outlived its usefulness

dog: Loyalty; family; base instincts, crudeness

doorknob: A potential for a new beginning that requires action

dragon: Magic; mystery; fierce protection; sexual energy; danger

dress: Traditional roles for women such as wife or mother; a profession

egg: New beginnings; fertility; creation and creativity, a project that is ready to begin

elephant: Memory; reverence of ancestors or elders; a project or promise that cannot be pushed aside

eye: Awareness; protection from evil; accusation

fan: A need to put more energy behind a transformation

feather: Intuition; air; the intellect; gentleness, a light touch; not taking things too seriously

fire: Change; devastation, destruction before renewal; passion; anger; South

fish: Knowledge; going with the flow; being surrounded by emotion or creativity; losing perspective

flags: Nationality; travel to distant lands

flower: Femininity; fertility; divinity, offerings, sacrifice; a specific season if you can identify the flower; its colors can also be interpreted in conjunction with this symbol

food: Fulfillment; offerings to ancestors or divinity; power. Can also be an indicator of the seasons: for example a turkey is commonly associated with Thanksgiving and candy with Halloween

foot: Travel; bare can represent reverence, sensitivity, a need for grounding

forearm: A disembodied forearm can represent emotional vulnerability and openness to interaction

goat: Male sexuality; versatility; resilience, stubbornness in arguments

graduation cap: Scholastic achievement; leadership; upward mobility in society

gun: Determination toward a goal; elimination of negativity; destruction; preparedness

hand: Spirituality; generosity; hobbies, hard work. A hand's actions are most telling: held up indicates stopping, held out while wearing a glove indicates accepting pay for hard labor

hat: A new leadership role to be taken on—the type of hat can indicate a professional or personal role

head: Note the facial expression, as it may be a about feelings that should be associated with other symbols. Can sometimes indicate a real person, so make sure to observe he hair and eye color plus any other distinguishing characteristics so the person could be identified later

heart: Love, emotion, passion; if the heart shape is broken or pierced, vulnerability

hips: Human hips relate to sexuality and physicality

horn: If filled with coins or other objects, a horn can be like a cornucopia. If it looks like a musical horn, it can represent a call to action or that somebody played a musical instrument in the past and needs an outlet for creativity at this time

horse: Loyalty; strength; travel over land

horseshoe: Good luck when the curve points downward and a lack of good luck when the curve points upward

house: Stability; family; self-imprisonment. Pay attention to the house's features—it might be a literal house

key: An initiator or catalyst to action; a secret that is locked away

keyhole: Over-specificity; pickiness; high standards for a lover; job opportunities that are not a match

knife: The intellect; cutting away old negativity to allow better things to come about in the future

lantern: A way in the darkness; leading a person out of a dark place; creative expression; an exit from loneliness

leaf: Temporary growth; impermanence; fragility, vulnerability; an indicator of the season or a vision's location

legs: Journey; emotional connection to others through effort; waiting (if the legs appear stationary); sexuality *lightning:* Unsettling and jarring change; unpleasant but necessary transformation; lack of support

lion: Strength, bravery; dangerous authority; opposition from a person in a place of power

lobster: The moon; cycles; the divine feminine; fear; water; emotion

mask: Hidden identity or emotions; protection against attack of a social or spiritual kind

monster: Inner conflict; a person's hidden personality; a demand for recognition; the monster's color can indicate more about its nature

moon: The divine feminine; magic; repeating cycles; fertility. Waning means gradually fading negativity or energy; waxing means the building of the energy, a new beginning

moth: Mystery; transformation; fear of the unknown; oddity

mouse: Details, potentially overlooking a treasure because it seems insignificant

mountain: A large obstacle; the higher self; climbing to a higher place in life; ambitions. Can represent real terrain, such as on a map, for instance

mouth: Communication of a message; warnings, dangers; mouth's expression can indicate the nature of the message

mushroom: Feeding off the energy of others; a lack of independence; possible substance abuse *musical instrument:* Can represent an actual instrument the person played in the past; a need for creative expression

musical note: A love of music; a message about love; spirituality; emotions that cannot be expressed in words

pen: A written message, especially the potential of a book or poetry

person: People can represent individuals in real life you are about to meet if you do not recognize them: postures or style of dress can be clues about the person's symbolic meaning

pyramid: Stability of the emotions and spirit; amplification of energy

rabbit: Fertility and abundance; possibly a message that a baby is on the way

rings: Marriage, the cycles of loyalty and desire for space in committed relationships

rock: A need for grounding, foundation, and/or stability; a cracked rock can indicate major instability, especially financially or in a friendship

rocket: Ambitions that have to be followed before stalled plans blow up

rolling pin: Efforts to make somebody conform to an ideal, most often that of a family member or authority figure

rope: Binding or entrapment (sometimes self-inflicted) but often imposed by a loved one

scythe: Endings, death; cutting away the old in order to make way for the new, harvesting; quitting while you're ahead

seashell: Femininity; love and creativity in the face of destructive emotional force

seed: A new beginning, potential creativity, a seasonal clue that could indicate a time frame if you watch the seed grow into something that appears in your life

seedlings: When growing upright can look like wands, so pay attention to the numbers and how they might represent barriers or energetic interventions in your life (refer to the symbolism of numbers earlier)

shepherd's crook: Guidance; spiritual forgiveness; gentleness

shield: Protection, defense in the midst of a battle; taking up a responsibility that puts you in the forefront of the attention of those in power

shoe: Travel; a role represented by the style of shoe; searching for a job

shoulders: Emotional passion and expression of body language

signpost: Journey; attention-seeking

skeleton: Death, needing to clear away old baggage keeping the full truth hidden

snake: Life and death; healing; danger versus peace

snowflake: Originality; creativity; cruelty; purity; wintertime; emotions that are unchanging *spade:* Intelligence; communication; battles to be fought; digging deeper into an issue; planting new seeds; building a strong foundation

spider: Community; deceit; protection of the home

square: Stability; conservative decisions regarding finances and social aspirations

star: Hopes, dreams; protection; earth; material things; friendships

strawberry: Summer; sensuality; rewards that are generous and pleasurable

sun: Growth; harmony; potential to being burned out if too much is done at once

sword: Conflict; intelligence; communication, talking over the telephone or by Internet, talking to somebody new

table: The home, a safe location; stability underneath a plan for financial gain or business

texture: If you see textured colors and abstractions, it can represent a desire for emotional closeness

thimble: Details; protection; minor dangers in life

torso: The home of the heart; nourishment and nurturing; emotional expressions of love

toy: Simplicity; harmlessness; phoniness

tower: Imprisonment, jail; poor judgment and foundations; someone getting payback or comeuppance for a wrongdoing *tree:* Family; nationality; roots that are deep in your past; a seasonal indicator

triangle: Moving from instability to stability after growth; possibly an arrow; getting together with others who share your goals to build strength of purpose

turkey: Thanksgiving; a clumsy and clueless person

uniform: A role in a career, often the identifying factor when seeing a person; for example a ghost may appear in uniform in order to point out that he or she was in the military in life

wall: A barrier to progress—note whether the wall seems suitable to vault, go around, or break through

wand: Fire; South; taking action; dynamic energy; sex, passion; a wand can appear as poles or sticks—this symbol is very flexible and frequently seen

water: Emotions; West; death; dream state; illusions

well: Deep emotions hidden or kept under control through force of will or secrecy

wing: Extra energy—note whether the wings are working in tandem or one is working harder than the other, representing the balance of energy in a relationship or group project

wolf: Sacred spirituality; protection, strength; danger; community

wood: Nature; flimsiness, phoniness

Exercises

1. Would you call yourself a "psychic," "clairvoyant," "intuitive," or a "fortune-teller?" Why would you choose that title? Why might you reject the other titles? Write down your response.

2. Share a symbol from your clairvoyant dictionary and its personal meaning with somebody else. Discuss how the symbol might differ between you, and what other symbols might be the same for both of you.

Theory

Clairvoyant Psychic Readings for a Purpose

"Reading for a purpose" means that you're going to be looking for information that will actually help your life. And *that* means you should focus on your goals and seeing those turning points that will help you best achieve them. When posing a question about a specific purpose, be careful how you phrase it; you need to be more involved and ask what *you* can do. Involve yourself in the question and ask for guidance. In this part of the chapter, I'll focus on asking the right questions, but there are some tips you should know going in. The most important of these tips is to remember to record your answers, even if they are negative or nonsensical.

When you start doing clairvoyant readings for specific purposes rather than just practicing your art, the stakes are much higher. Chances are, there are sights you will *want* to see, and those might differ from the things you actually will see. You will be tempted to do another clairvoyant reading on the same question, with the hope that your first vision was wrong or confused. Avoid the temptation to repeat readings on the same topic so soon.

Remember when I told you that your destiny was like a network of roads? When you do the same reading twice, you might see all the other options out there. That doesn't necessarily help you to find out how to get where you're going, and it may simply confuse you since different answers may well be contradictory. Instead, record the very first answer you get, no matter how silly or sad. Then, work to make a choice about the topic at hand. After you have actually made a choice and implemented your change, you can perform another clairvoyant reading for help.

There are quite a few clients of my fortune-telling business who get stuck in the rut of requesting more readings until they get the answers they like. One, for example, wants to marry a specific man who has stated that he is not interested in her. During clairvoyant visioning, I saw him and a future in which he was never getting married. I looked for her turning point and saw that the best course of action for her would be to quit pining for him and to open herself up to a new relationship. Only in that way would she be able to maintain his friendship and also marry somebody else.

Well, the client wanted another reading right away. I asked her if she had cut off contact with him, and she admitted that she had not. Indeed, nothing about the way she was dealing with him and her love life had changed at all. I politely declined to read for her until she had made a decision to do things differently, whether that meant taking my advice to cut off contact, or trying a drastic new solution of her own like proposing marriage or sleeping with his best friend or whatever she wanted to do with her free will. As I pointed out, another reading would at best be a waste of her money if I saw the same vision again. At worst, it would result in confusing and contradictory advice as more and more remote and unfortunate possibilities would appear.

And that story brings us to the first of our topics for readings: love. Love is by far the most frequent topic brought up when clients come to me for fortune-telling. It can also be a challenge to perform a clairvoyant reading on your own love life because of the bias you naturally have toward wishing your hopes and dreams come true without seeing that you could have an even better future on a different course. Like the client I mentioned above, you can easily turn your head away from the best outcome when you have the blinders of love on your face. For that reason it is very important to ask the right questions, record the first answers you get, and for goodness sake, take action to change the patterns in your life.

Love

Imagine a client whom I will call Sandy. On the outside, Sandy seemed pretty well put together. She had a dynamite career as a sales representative for a major movie production company, she already owned her own home at the age of twenty-six, and she had a beautiful son who was just starting at an expensive and prestigious private school. The one thing that Sandy did not have going for her was a romantic relationship.

Sandy had spent her entire adult life in an on-again off-again relationship with her son's father, whom she still loved dearly. Aside from that, she had dated a long string of men who simply did not meet her high standards. Sandy was a busy woman, and she felt like she didn't have time to waste on men who were not right for her and not daddy material for her boy. Besides, she had already invested so much time and emotion in her ex, and she didn't want to quit until it was over for certain.

When I performed a clairvoyant reading for Sandy, I described her ex perfectly, as he was on the forefront of her mind. Using a crystal ball, I saw a face before my eyes of a man older than Sandy who had swarthy skin and dark hair. I saw a baseball cap with a symbol on it on his head, and I paused to tell Sandy that the cap might be a symbol for a role in life that he had taken on, but Sandy enthusiastically told me that it matched the description of his favorite team cap that he frequently wore.

With a fair amount of hope, I looked for some symbols of the marriage for which Sandy yearned, searching the crystal ball for images of bells, the two of them embracing, or other wedding imagery. Instead, I saw him standing on a bridge refusing to cross one way or another, keeping Sandy on the unstable wooden slats over rushing water as she tried to coax him across. The metaphor was not promising, and I pointed this out to a clearly disappointed Sandy. Undeterred, she asked if there was any chance of the two of them getting together.

I asked her if that was what she really wanted. She just sat and shrugged miserably. "What do you want and need?" I asked. All she needed, she said, was a loving companion for herself and a stable family for her son. She was just hoping that her ex would be a part of that vision. Looking again into the crystal ball, I saw another man whom she was embracing, this one much more slender than the last, though of a similar complexion. Other images swirled around, a guitar with musical notes and a work glove holding a coin and a flag. I told Sandy that those symbols might mean that he is of a different nationality, he might play guitar, and he might work with his hands to earn a living.

Sandy left my office that day grateful that someone else had given her other options besides putting all her efforts into pursuing her ex. Later, she happily reported back that she was connecting with a new man who matched the description in the reading. This boyfriend, having kids from a previous marriage himself, was just as happy as she to form a stable family.

When constructing love questions, it will be difficult to think clearly about your true goals. The vast majority of my clients have love questions about specific people, hoping for a love connection, despondent with no other potential solutions if the answer is simply negative. I'll show you some of the poorly worded questions I usually receive, along with some better questions that can be asked instead. And even these questions can be transformed into the very best questions, the ones most likely to be answered in your clairvoyant reading.

Good love questions
Can I see the face or initials of a
good potential for my next relationship?
No matter how down in the dumps you may feel about love, most of you out there are probably not looking at a situation

in which there is only *one* potential person left in the world for you to date. Acknowledging that there are multiple potentials allows you to start thinking in terms of controlling your own choices and thus, your destiny.

If my goal is reunion with my ex,
what can I do to best bring about my goal?
Even if you are hoping against hope, try to focus on your desired outcome and what path—no matter how difficult—you should take to maximize your chances of getting there.

I am choosing between two people. May I see
the face or name of the one who is best for me?
Narrowing down your choices doesn't mean your clairvoyance is any less amazing; it may help clarify what you actually want.

Best love questions
What should I be thinking about in
order to draw the best love match for me?
Empowering yourself to be the attracting factor when finding new love is a great way to build confidence and increase your chances of success. A clairvoyant reading on this question may show you behaving and appearing in ways that will help you, or it may reveal symbolic suggestions for improving personal traits.

What sorts of signs should I be looking for when
asking whether a person is marriage material for me?
This question formation makes use of the potential for omens to be given to you when somebody with the right traits comes along.

What can I do to help my relationship improve?
This question is pretty vague, but in a good way because it focuses on an outcome and the way you can bring it about.

What not to say
Is my ex going to come back to me?
Obviously, the answer is most likely going to be no, and such a question usually leaves no other options but to be upset or to lie to oneself about the answer.

Am I going to get married?
If marriage is your goal, it is pretty silly to try seeing if you can achieve that goal without first deciding how you are going to get there or without working towards it. You are in control of your own destiny, so even if the answer was yes, you could turn around and join a celibate holy order the next day if you wanted to, refusing the potential future you saw. You could certainly complain that the clairvoyant reading was wrong, but you can see how you'd only have yourself to blame.

Who is my soul mate?
It is a common misconception that there is one soul mate perfectly matched for each person on the planet. It is a further misconception that once one meets up with a soul mate, the two will be together indefinitely. Very often, people have choices between several significant others who will make an important mark on each others' lives. And some will have a succession of such remarkable people.

Money

One of my clients is a family man, let's call him Chris, who has had ups and downs with money his entire life. He cut up his credit cards because he was too scared to use them, for fear of getting into debt, but he is never too tight on cash to the point of being unable to afford readings. I always tell him that, if things get too tight, he should be focusing on working hard for his family rather than getting clairvoyant readings. However, his work is freelance, which makes his income unpredictable.

When he came to me after meeting with his accountant, asking whether he would be able to pay for his eldest child's college the next year, I urged him to think about his goal in other ways. He had a child he wanted to put through college, and it honestly didn't matter where the money might come from. In my visions, I saw a few of the jobs that he could do in order to bring in the most income. I also saw more symbolic imagery of a treasure chest, which we both took to mean locking up his savings so he couldn't spend it on other things.

In the end, I saw a wonderful image of his child with a graduation cap that was encouraging to both of us. He was already urging his kids to apply for scholarships when they went to college, so we knew that, no matter what the source, graduation was a realizable dream. For Chris, that helped him work harder and save more without feeling like it all might be wasted.

Of course, being a clairvoyant doesn't make you a qualified financial planner. Even when all is going as it should, a lot of money decisions are left to chance, giving people a lot of leeway to include clairvoyance in their financial decisions along with other more traditional advisers. The benefit of clairvoyance is that it's possible to see actual numbers. However, in my experience those numbers can sometimes be jumbled, so they certainly aren't anything to make plans or place bets upon. Just as it is hard to read in your dreams because the symbolic left brain is working more than the analytical right brain, your clairvoyant visions may easily mess up the order of numbers and letters.

Good money questions

Can I expect an increase in pay
if I look for another job right now?
This question examines the potential outcome of a specific action, which is a great way to use your clairvoyant abilities. Use your sight to investigate what your life would be like under specific circumstances, and then decide if the outcome is acceptable to you.

Of two potential price points, which
should I choose when listing my house?
Narrowing down your potential options is a good way to figure out which path to take. When asking such a question, you might see the outcome of your life after choosing either option, or you might see specific numbers that give you a more precise answer.

When is the best time to make a major purchase?
Another benefit of the ability to see numbers in clairvoyant visions is that you can alter the timing of your decisions. This sort of question is particularly good if you already know that you are going to take a particular course of action, but you're procrastinating until the time is right. Keep in mind that if you

see a number, it may be a digit in the date or a specific number of days, weeks, months, or even years. You can be more specific if you want to clear that up. For example, "How many years until…"

Best money questions
What can I do to improve the chances
of earning more money at my present job?
This sort of question outlines what limits you desire, such as keeping a comfortable job, while specifying an attainable goal and looking for the turning points needed in order to get there.

What should I be thinking about in order
to make my life more financially stable?
Often it isn't a specific financial goal one has in mind, but rather an essential core value. If there are far too many things that need fixing in your financial life, think about your central need, such as stability, and speak to that. Your visions can guide you to a better future.

I have a goal to go on an expensive vacation
next year. What can I do to achieve my goal?
For any dream that requires financial input you can start focusing on that goal and visualizing the outcome. When your clairvoyant visions kick in, you may see some excellent ways to get started on that goal, even if they are just tiny steps that you can take the first day you think about it.

What not to say

What are the winning lotto numbers?

If clairvoyants could know the winning lotto numbers, I'd be too busy rolling in money to write this book for you right now. Numbers can be switched around in the visions, or, more likely, the emotional stakes may be just too high to be able to have a clear head when trying to see winning lotto numbers. This is why successful stories of psychic help for this question are rare.

In which stocks should I invest?

This is a question better aimed at a qualified financial planner than a clairvoyant! The letters of stock names can be switched around in your head just as easily as numbers.

Will I be rich someday?

Again, this question focuses on a yes or a no without putting you in charge. Even if the answer were yes, you know that you could easily throw all the money away or refuse to put in the work to get it. Similarly, people can change their negative outlook. If you have a goal of being rich, try instead to identify the means to achieving this goal.

Career

Quite a few of my clients are realtors. The unpredictable feast-or-famine nature of the real estate industry tends to draw such people to clairvoyants, hoping for a peek at the future. One of my clients whom I'll call Ann, was constantly moving elements of her career around like chess pieces, trying to move herself upward in the world, even though she was already highly successful in her career as a realtor. She had a knack for social interactions. When Ann was in the room, you felt like she knew you as a friend and that she was giving you her undivided attention despite her telephone's headset blinking on one ear and the business text messages lighting up her purse.

However, Ann confessed that she was a terrible judge of character. In the sea of home buyers in which she was constantly swimming, she could never realize when she was wasting an entire afternoon showing a bored couple around who never intended to buy. She also had the unpleasant task of working to promote herself as a realtor through advertising and maintaining a business website, blog, and social media presence. Ann felt as if she had a full-time job as a small business owner as well as a full-time job in her chosen career, and it was confusing and exhausting having to wear so many hats.

My sessions with Ann were easy for the both of us because she came armed with questions about people, and I came prepared to see and describe faces and symbols surrounding people so she could pick them out. Ann would ask who might be the best buyer for a specific house, and I would allow myself to see a vision and then describe a family, a couple, or for example, a man with a jutting chin and graying hair. Never one to waste opportunities, Ann scribbled down these descriptions in a notebook, even if she recognized who I was talking about right away. When asking about hiring or firing decisions for marketing partners, I would see people, describe the right ones, and then let her know if I saw positive or negative signs around them. Ann, as organized as she was, would note down a bright green check mark for yes, and a red X for no.

Good career questions
What sort of job should I be seeking?

Clairvoyance is a wonderful tool because it can show you symbols of the sort of job that would suit you or your lifestyle well at this point in time. You might see a vision of your actual workplace, or you might see some tools of the trade, or symbols of the products or services provided.

What should I do to avoid getting fired?

If you value your job but feel that the winds are changing, you can make it your goal to avoid being fired and then search for visions that show you what to do. Everything you do can change your destiny. Even if it is a long shot, you can try your best and know that you did everything possible in order to keep your job.

Should I take a job I've been offered,
or hold out for something better?

Another benefit of clairvoyance is your ability to see your life's outcomes on varied paths. So you can visualize yourself on the path of a new job and then pause to visualize what your life would be like if you kept on working your way up the ladder at your current job. This sort of question examines forks in your path that can be adapted to many scenarios.

Best career questions
What sort of personal strengths of mine should I
be thinking about when searching for a job?

As predictable as it may be, this question is a good one because it works. That's why high school guidance counselors have been asking their students this question for generations. Your clairvoyance can help you see past any low self-esteem or delusions of grandeur to see clearly your true strengths, instead of those you simply wish you have.

I have a goal of career stability.
What should I do to achieve my goal?
Set a clear value statement, such as stability, flexibility and freedom, wealth, power, fame, and prestige. Once you've decided what your goals are in a career, you can begin seeing some visions about what you have to do. This question is a good one because it doesn't matter how fantastically great or mediocre the outcome may be. You can still have clairvoyant visions that will move you in the right direction.

Can I be shown some people who may
be able to help me get or keep a good career?
Make full use of your clairvoyant skill to see peoples' faces, names, and places of business. Encouraging your clairvoyant self to see literal visions of the future can help you focus, especially if you tend to get too many cryptic symbols when you have a vision.

What not to say
Will I get a job?
A simplistic question like this one places the power out of your hands; thus the answer is quite clear *and* vague at the same time. If the answer is yes, you know you can't just sit inside an apartment all day playing video games and not looking for work. If the answer is no, would you just give up on life? A

more productive question gives you a course of action to move toward the destiny you desire.

Am I going to be happy in my career?
It is good to make happiness a goal in any sector of your life, but you'll have to be more specific about what you need to be happy, and then look for what you have to do in order to get there. Think about what constitutes a happy career life and ask to see what will be conducive to reaching that goal.

Am I going to get fired?
Again, this question focuses on an external locus of control, in this case whether the world will see fit to fire you from your job or not. Fear of being fired is a valid concern, but to frame the question more productively, you'll have to decide whether you would prefer to stay in your job or to secure another one before getting fired, and then look for signs of what you should do in order to achieve that goal.

Family

When a client I'll call Julie came to me at a psychic fair for a clairvoyant reading regarding family matters, it turned out to be a rather more intimate session than seemed possible in the busy, public environment. We started off talking about her relationship with her father, which was strained even at the best of times, and the condition of her grandmother. She was already aware that her grandmother was dying, and was comforted by a vision I had where she and her father would be able to talk and become closer during the process of her grandmother's death.

Feeling encouraged by the clairvoyant reading, Julie briefly left my booth to fetch her husband for another question. They had been trying to have a child for years, but she was in her forties and he in his fifties, so fertility was an issue. They were just starting to work with a fertility specialist in a process of elimination that might lead to expensive treatments.

I listened to their story patiently, but explained that my clairvoyant visions might see the faces of children acquired through adoption, or even godchildren, nieces or nephews. Julie had tears in her eyes as she bobbed her head in understanding. Her husband had a youthful twinkle in his own, but a shock of white hair and a tired expression. My vision, however, showed a little baby girl as well as showing Julie pregnant, much to her joy. I remember that occasion specifically, because she joyously proclaimed on the spot that she was going to name her daughter after me as I gave her my business card to keep in touch. It turned out to be a pretty good lifelong connection for one made at a little psychic fair.

Good family questions

Can you tell me about my future children?
Though clairvoyance is not a very precise pregnancy diagnostic tool, it can help you to tell you about what your future family potential can be. You can have strong visions of your future children as well as symbols that represent their personalities. Asking the question in this open format also allows for visions of children that enter your life through other means such as adoption, family ties, or close friendships that form bonds that are like parent to child.

What can I do in order to best try to have
a better relationship with an estranged relative?
Acknowledging that you are only one half of the equation, this question empowers you with the ability to do whatever actions that will best promote harmony between you and a relative, nothing more or less. When you have clairvoyant visions about your future with the relative, take care to notice what *you* are doing in the visions rather than what the relative is doing so you will know what actions to take.

How can I support quality and
quantity of life for my dying relative?
We all want to see our loved ones last, and watching some-body age or die is a helpless feeling. Focus on what you can do instead of external events. It may be that you simply see yourself talking with and spending quality time with your rel-ative, bringing cheer to the person's final days. Or, you could see something that could cause you to want to consult with his or her doctors. Either way, try to take a positive outlook.

Best family questions
How can I be a better parent?
There is no such thing as the perfect parent, but we could all use some improvement. If you are planning a larger fam-ily or thinking about getting sterilized after having kids, this question can also help you confirm your decision if you have visions of your future with your family looking the same or different than it does now. This open-ended question allows your visions to show you a snapshot of family life or a deeper, more philosophical message.

*How can I feel more content
with my family relationships?*

Sometimes we struggle with one family member because of deeper issues than just our relationship with that family member. If nothing can be done to resolve a past childhood event or the way that you interact with a certain gender, perhaps your clairvoyant visions can instead show you how you can interact with a specific relative as a person.

*What should I be thinking about regarding my
dying relative, for the best of all concerned?*

If you're dealing with end-of-life issues for somebody, or if you are not sure whether your relative wants to extend his or her life, it can be safer to allow your clairvoyant visions to show you the most important thing you need to see about the issue. Before you ask such questions, be sure that you are ready to see what you need to see. If you are not prepared to lose someone, or if you have your heart set on a specific outcome, seeing otherwise may be disturbing.

What not to say

Am I pregnant?

If you put yourself out there as a clairvoyant, you will encounter this question frequently. If you are planning a family, you'll wonder this question yourself. However, clairvoyance is not a necessary or sufficient diagnostic tool. The spiritual and symbolic significance of "pregnancy" means that you can see visions that indicate a false positive or negative quite easily.

Will I ever fix my relationship
with an estranged relative?
It is hard when two family members are at odds, and when you remember that your estranged family member has free will and his or her own life to lead, that can make it more frustrating. However, you can reframe these questions in a way that empowers you without infringing upon another person's free will by thinking about what you need socially and what you believe you are not getting from that family member.

When is my elderly relative going to die?
Clairvoyance is often consulted in order to see death, and there are many stories of people who have seen the demise of loved ones before it happens. However, there is much in the environment alone we cannot control, and your loved one can certainly make choices to change destiny. Before asking about death, think about why you are doing so. Is your question about preparing yourself, or is it about changing what you think is the future?

Health

I don't do clairvoyant health readings *unless* I am contacted after a person has already been to the proper health professionals. Luckily, since one of my offices is inside of a wellness center, it is easy to verify whether the client has sought proper help in addition to a clairvoyant reading. Most often, I find myself faced with somebody who is waiting for the results of a test to come through and would like a glimpse of his or her future in the meantime. When one of my clients came to me, she was waiting for a number of such tests.

This client was experiencing kidney failure and was going through many tests, but the one that presently worried her happened to be an HIV test. Nobody wants to think about the possibility of dying of AIDS, and all the testing surrounding her potential transplant readiness were bringing up all sorts of anxieties that might have never crossed her mind otherwise. Was a lover she'd had decades ago potentially a carrier? I felt uncomfortable giving her a clairvoyant reading since I can't diagnose the presence of any disease, however, I did offer to see if I could see any visions of her future.

Luckily for my client, I did have a vision of her receiving a transplant from a living donor, because she was undertaking activities in my visions that would have been impossible for her to accomplish in her present state of health. Years later, the client returned to me to confirm the accuracy of my vision. Of course, I did nothing for her except give her peace of mind and a positive vision of her own to hold in her mind for the future. When facing a serious health problem, sometimes a positive attitude and visualization are the most important benefits received from clairvoyance.

Good health questions

*I have been presented a choice between two
treatment options. Which should I choose?*

In conjunction with health care, clairvoyant visions can be very helpful. I have used them myself during major decisions about my own breast tumors, kidney disease, and giving birth to my children. Often, your medical team will explain to you the benefits and drawbacks between two courses of action, and leave you to decide between the lesser of two evils. At this point, a clairvoyant vision can be used. If you have a hard time visualizing the two options, you might just assign each one a number and then ask for one of the numbers to be presented to you during your vision.

How can I motivate myself to make healthy
changes in my nutrition or lifestyle?
Another case in which clairvoyant visions can be helpful is when the doctors have already told you the right thing to do, but it is simply too challenging for you to undertake. Most likely, this is an exercise protocol or a stringent diet. You can seek in your clairvoyant visions to see what will motivate you. Whether it be exciting new dance lessons or locks on the cupboards, make sure that you honor what your visions have shown you, if they are in line with your doctor's advice.

How can I improve my
emotional health and attitude?
Often we're just stuck with a chronic health condition for life, and that is just no fun. At that point, emotional health and well-being can suffer, which is easily exacerbated by a negative outlook on life. In your readings, focus on ways to improve your attitude. This attacks a problem you can control directly, and you can turn your life around in a positive way.

Best health questions
What should I be focusing on with regard
to improving my well-being and health?
If everything is going fairly well in your life and you are already discussing any problems with a doctor, you can

address your health status in a clairvoyant reading by asking what your focus should be. At times, mental and emotional health are more important than physical, which may be indicated through visions of social interactions.

What adjunct practices in addition
to my healthcare will improve my health?
Clairvoyant readings are only one practice that can be added on to improve your well-being. Through your visioning, you may be able to see other spiritual actions or hobbies that can bring about a deeper sense of peace, wellness and overall health.

What can I do to improve
my quality of life regardless of health?
Sometimes we just get dealt a bad genetic hand, and health problems are just part of the game of life. Instead of focusing on your dismal health destiny, let your doctors worry about managing any diseases and use your clairvoyant abilities to find out how to transcend your problems. You might find that creative or spiritual activities may be indicated in your visions, to bring you out of a funk induced by chronic pain or illness.

What not to say
Am I going to die?
A pretty common question for psychics over the ages, of course you realize by now that it ignores the role you play in changing your own destiny. A false answer could be devastating, so think about why you want to ask the question. Do you need to make plans? Are you suffering from irrational fears? Do you just have a morbid sense of curiosity? These feelings can be explored through more constructive ways than clairvoyant visioning.

Should I go to the doctor?
Clairvoyance is *not* a substitute for consulting a qualified medical practitioner. Even the most gifted clairvoyant, able to see what medical imaging machines cannot, would still be unqualified to diagnose or treat any disease. If there is any question at all that you might need to see a doctor, please save yourself some time and confusion—consult your doctor first.

What is going on with my health?
Again, if you have no idea what is going on with your health, a clairvoyant vision may be as confusing as staring at a technical diagram of an ultrasound. You'd do better to leave the diagnostics to doctors, and focus your health questions on things that you can do to improve your life.

Clairvoyant Séances

A séance is one way a clairvoyant can communicate with the dead. The idea behind a séance is that a group of people, all desiring to contact the same ghost and all having agreed on the same questions to ask, will come together to share their energy and their clairvoyant visions. If you are the only clairvoyant you know, a séance is one way that others can benefit from the skills that you have developed. If, however, you are acquainted with more than one clairvoyant, a séance is a way for everyone to pool their talents and thereby gain the best clairvoyant experience possible.

As a beginning clairvoyant, don't expect a séance to feel any different from trance meditation or scrying. The extra benefits you'll receive here are the strong energies of intention that come from other people in the room, potentially helping your visions come faster. Also, you'll benefit from the interpretations that other people in the room share about what they see. You may be surprised at how your visions vary from other people who are sitting right next to you. The best way to go into a séance as a beginner is with the hope that you will help others at the séance with what clairvoyant abilities you have developed so far.

You will need:

1. Willing participants who are fully informed that they will be participating in a séance.

2. A table and chairs for all participants.

3. A divination tool for the center of the table. Traditionally this has been a crystal ball or a dark bowl of water with a few drops of oil added. You can use any scrying tool, but above all I recommended using the one that works best for you.

4. Your clairvoyant journal, so you can write down questions that were asked, and answers received.

Steps to a séance for beginners

1. Agree on what ghost to summon. As a beginner, it is best to only try for one ghost per session to avoid confusion. If the ghost doesn't come, enjoy some chit chat and snacks, call it a night, and try again another time.

2. Agree on what questions will be asked and who will ask them before starting the séance. Agree not to pipe up with any questions that were not figured out in advance. Some participants may not feel comfortable asking certain questions, and it is a violation of trust to shout out questions without thinking of the comfort levels of others. Decide how long people should meditate in between questions while waiting for an answer. Two to five minutes is a good amount of time for beginners.

3. Talk about grounding with everyone, and consider leading a grounding visualization. A good grounding suggestion for beginners is to have everyone take shoes and socks off and place bare feet on the floor, legs uncrossed, to allow the energy to flow downward naturally.

4. Everyone should sit around the table evenly spaced apart. Ideally the table would be circular, but you can make do with any configuration, as long as people can reach each other. Have each person place hands on the table palms down and slide hands forward until each pinky finger touches the pinky fingers of the people sitting to the left and to the right. At this point, a circle of energy should be formed between all participants. It should be announced that if anyone feels uncomfortable, he or she can withdraw hands, breaking the circle of energy to allow the séance to end.

5. Have one person request the presence of the chosen ghost out loud. Begin with everyone sitting in quiet, clear-headed meditation, controlling breathing to allow a trance state for all concerned. At any time, participants can open their eyes to gaze into the scrying tool at the center of the table. They can also keep their eyes closed for the entire session. After about two to five minutes, the asker can speak their question. Everyone should wait before the next question is asked. Anyone can take a break to write down answers that they receive. If people feel comfortable sharing aloud any clairvoyant visions, they can do so.

6. After the séance, debrief with everyone and take notes. Go around the circle and allow each person time to speak about what they saw, because some people might not want to speak up unless given a turn. By pooling everyone's experiences, you will be able to get a richer and more complete message from the summoned ghost. If any participants did not see anything at all, that is okay too. They can be assured that their energy helped the rest of the participants have a better chance at contacting the ghost in question.

Ethics

If you have been working hard at becoming a clairvoyant and beginning to see signs of success, by now you may begin to run into some questions of right and wrong you never thought would occur. After all, what is morally sketchy about having the

gift of clear sight? Well, it turns out that there are tricky problems that can surface when you are a clairvoyant. Many ethical
questions crop up because of how our society works. Issues of
privacy, etiquette, fraud, and potential pathology are common;
you'll have to check yourself for the presence and absence of
all of those things. How to do so? It's easiest to follow a code
of ethics, which may mean setting limits on your clairvoyant
practice, even if you believe it to be part of your religious cus-
tom or even your identity. The following section will go over
the most common ethical issues that may crop up for you.

"Knowing" what may not be ours to know

If you picked up this book, chances are you're the kind of person who loves to know everything about a situation before
taking action. Before you waste your time dating someone,
for example, you might prefer to know whether the person is a
real prospect for marriage. Perhaps you want to know whether
you are a good fit for a job before you even go to the interview.
Many people prefer not to know everything about life before
it happens, and it is a good idea to try to understand this perspective, not only to respect the wishes of others for whom you
might read, but also to gain this wisdom for yourself.

First, you'll have to figure out why you would even want
to use your clairvoyant abilities to look into the future. You will
get a hint as to how I feel personally from the section on asking the right questions in chapter 5. You will see that rather
than just looking at the future as something unchangeable, I
believe every choice changes the future. The goal of clairvoyance should be to see the true and best paths to take in order

to get closer to achieving the goal of living a blissful life. I may have presented this argument so convincingly that you readily agree. But you may still find it hard to resist the idea that clairvoyance shows a single true future, especially if you see things with your own eyes which raise your hopes or terrify you.

Those who don't want to see their future avoid clairvoyance all together, preferring only to see the final truth when it actually happens. Perhaps such people are under the mistaken impression that one can't change an unpleasant future seen in a clairvoyant vision. Or even more likely, they don't want to see something that could be disheartening or confusing. Knowing your own boundaries makes for wise clairvoyant practice, so I'd like to give you some advice on how to avoid the issues that make some people stop dealing with clairvoyance entirely.

How to see without being invasive

You don't have to swear off your clairvoyant practice forever if you are not in the mood to see a bad outcome, but you can certainly wait until you are in a better head space to do clairvoyant work, or you can reframe your question. Setting some limitations on when and why you practice clairvoyance can ensure that it is a healthy addition to your life, not a confusing obsession.

Before doing a clairvoyant reading on the future of a specific situation in your life, the first step is to ask yourself why you want to see the outcome of that particular scenario. Is it due to morbid curiosity, or do you have a desire to use your clairvoyant vision to take charge of your destiny? You can tell it is more likely the former when your questions tend to have a short and final answer. The only way to shake the feeling that external events are controlling your life is to reframe your question to give yourself the power, rather than passively viewing your life as if you were fast-forwarding to another part of a movie.

Secondly, ask yourself whether you are ready to see a negative potential outcome. In cases where somebody you love is sick and dying, or when a relationship is coming to an end, you might be in a vulnerable place emotionally. The last thing you need is to start living a visually torturous experience through clairvoyant readings before you have even begun mourning the loss.

Another situation in which you should avoid doing a reading is when you have your heart set on a specific future but are not willing to alter your path. What is the point of doing a clairvoyant reading if you don't want help going forward? For example, if you want to keep chasing an ex around who doesn't want to take you back, think about whether you are willing to stop or change your actions. If you will never stop pursuing the ex no matter what you see in your clairvoyant vision, don't bother doing a clairvoyant reading. After all, it will only make you depressed or angry if you see something you don't want to see. *Only* perform a clairvoyant reading if you are ready to make changes in your life based on what you see.

How to see for others AND mind your own business

Doing clairvoyant readings for others makes ethical boundaries even trickier. Obviously, you won't be doing many clairvoyant readings for people who don't want to know anything about their futures, though you might do readings that provide clarity about past and present decisions. However, if you aren't careful, you might find out embarrassing details about their lives and character flaws. Imagine doing a clairvoyant reading for your mom and seeing some sexual proclivities you wish you hadn't seen in the first place. Such things are obviously not what you intended!

Therefore, getting a topic of focus or a question from somebody can be very helpful before a reading clairvoyant readings moreso than in other types of psychic work. If the person chooses not to share a topic of focus or a question, you can limit yourself in your mind using your common sense. Limiting what you see is not easy, but that's why you've been practicing meditation. Just as, when you meditate, you allow extraneous thoughts to float away, you can allow visions you don't want to see to vanish, taking only casual note of them in passing. Concentrate on what you want to see. Draw out those visions, allowing any other flashes to subside without further inquiry.

Of course, controlling your own mind is easier said than done, especially if you are naturally snoopy like me. I've had moments in which I became aware of somebody's personal relationship problems when I was asked about a career problem, and I've seen minor legal issues a person was trying to hide. In those cases, it was none of my business, so I had to try not to pry or embarrass my clients. Sometimes, as with any other accidental discovery in life, the trick is knowing when to keep your mouth shut.

Whether to tell the person or not when you see something bad

Politeness may already have trained you to ignore when you observe something embarrassing, since that's not limited to clairvoyant experiences. For example, you might stifle a reaction when your boss farts in public or if you stumble across a roommate's porn stash. But it is much more difficult to ignore a frightening message for somebody. If you see the death or serious injury of a person in a clairvoyant reading, it may become an ethical quandary. Is it worse to watch the person die without warning him or her? Or is it worse to invade privacy and possibly alienate a friend by freaking him or her out?

If you do choose to tell a person about a clairvoyant vision, it should only be somebody who has requested a clairvoyant reading or has at least given his or her consent. For example you might say, "I had a dream about your future last night. May I tell you about it?" Even when the reading is requested, don't share something terrifying and negative unless the person says he or she is ready to hear bad news and you believe him or her. Use your common sense and watch for emotional body language, such as signs of imminent crying or the crossing of arms or legs, which may warn you to back off.

Here's a good story about holding off on a reading's results because the audience was not ready: I was hired as a psychic for a little girl's slumber party, hosted by her parents. It was a lot of fun! I taught the kids how to read tea leaves and did tarot readings for them, mainly on the topics of school and boys. During the course of the party, one of the girls asked me if her father was going to get healthier. At that moment, I had a vision about her father becoming very ill, having to undergo cancer treatments, and dying. Can you imagine how disastrous it would have been if I had told the little girl this news at a slumber party? I told her it was something she should talk about with her family, and that things like these were not in our control. Then I changed the subject to something more positive she could control in her life.

Now, I'm not saying you should never share bad news. I had seen a vision of a good friend of mine, also in a hospital bed, and I knew that it was something fatal, like cancer. Since he was a pretty strong, confident, and self-actualized person, I asked him if he was ready to hear something terrible in a vision. He knew it was serious because there were tears in my eyes. I told him about my vision and he said that maybe it was a good thing that whatever illness was seen was caught early enough for treatment. Two years later I thought of him out of the blue and had a vision of him in a hospital again. Worried, I called him and asked him to tell me what was going on. He told me that he had just been diagnosed with aggressive mantle cell lymphoma, and was thankful that it had been discovered in time for equally aggressive treatment.

There are several reasons why it might be better not to tell a person what you see in a case like this. First of all, you just might be wrong. I had a horrific vision once of a boyfriend's death, and it freaked me out terribly. I thought that he would be, in very short order, gone from my life. I described to him the odd waking nightmare in which I saw him die in a rainstorm. He was not afraid, because he knew I was going through some serious mental and emotional issues at the time. If you look back at my list of symbols, you will see that water is a symbol for emotions and death or endings. This can put a less literal spin on the meaning of a vision. At the time, I was feeling so overwhelmed by emotions that I was afraid that my meltdown would end my relationship. I was lucky that he was skeptical. If he had believed me, you can see how it may have limited his life, causing him always to avoid driving in the rain. I'm happy to report that ten years later, he is still alive and kicking—and goes out into rainstorms with impunity.

Another reason not to deliver bad news is that it is simply rude to do so against a person's will. Even if you are the type of person who wants to know everything, remember that there are others who do not want to know what lies ahead, fearing that it will make for a life filled with boredom or dread.

Ruining life's surprises

Keeping a bit of perspective will help you to avoid the feeling that clairvoyance ruins the surprises in life. And you will have to consciously communicate that perspective when reading for others. Never forget that some people may think that clairvoyance endows you with the ability to see everything and anything in the future exactly as it plays out, as if you were omniscient. You will have to remind each person for whom you read that no matter what you see, he or she will still be in charge of his or her own destiny. Here is how you might phrase things:

1. "I see you kissing a blond man. Remember, he may be one out of many potential boyfriends you can choose."

2. "I see you working at a new job as a construction supervisor. Remember, you'll still have to work hard to find and get this job if you want it, and you can always choose another path."

3. "I see you taking off your wedding ring and divorcing your husband. But obviously this is in your control. It is up to you to decide if and when you've had enough, and my vision just confirms that you have the option of ending the marriage."

Above all, never pressure anyone to have a clairvoyant reading who is frightened about what you might see, even if you can sense that it will be good news. Respecting somebody's privacy sometimes means taking every measure available, that is, not pushing the subject at all. Even if you think your friend is burying her head in the sand, you could easily jeopardize your friendship by forcing her out of her comfort zone. It is best to respect others' beliefs.

Clairvoyance and You: Potential Problems

Being a clairvoyant is a completely natural skill that anyone can have. Why, then, don't we all use this skill and talk about clairvoyance in everyday life? Our culture is why. In our society, we have a lot of criteria that determine when and under what conditions people might have spiritual experiences, especially when literal visions are involved. As such, there are a lot of ways that you can trip up and violate social rules. You could get into trouble, even lose your friends or ruin your life. Here are a few ways that you can take your clairvoyant practice too far.

Gambling

If clairvoyance could help somebody see the winning lottery numbers, timing on a slot machine, or poker hand, I would be too busy rolling in my winnings to be able to write this book! Unfortunately, belief in clairvoyance can be one way that people end up forming gambling addictions. As you develop your clairvoyant practice, especially if you see imagery related to gambling, you may find yourself becoming tempted to gamble, using your clairvoyant visions to inform your guesses.

Remember that there may be many reasons why your clairvoyant visions don't work. Numbers can be mixed up in your visions, timing may be off, you might see a potential future that never manifests. Or, you might simply be mistaking your own wishful thinking for a clairvoyant vision.

To take the point further, how would you tell that your clairvoyant beliefs are turning into a problem? If you find yourself hiding your clairvoyant beliefs when it comes to gambling, this is one sign that might indicate a problem. After all, if your clairvoyant abilities were really helpful when you gamble, you'd be shouting it from the rooftops. Obviously you have a problem if you gamble when the money is not there, if you realize that gambling affects your life in a negative way, or if your friends start to worry about you. If at any point you have an issue with gambling, seek help as with any addiction. Do not use clairvoyance to try to solve the problem.

Scaring people

Being clairvoyant can be pretty exciting at first, especially if you start to have some success and begin reading for others. I'll admit that I've enjoyed the attention I've received from clients, family, and friends during clairvoyant readings. There's no doubt that you'll get even more amazed reactions and riveted stares if you give very good or very bad news. It is important to consider whether you're being overly dramatic when you deliver your clairvoyant readings.

As was mentioned before, you should never push a clairvoyant reading on somebody who doesn't want one, for any reason. If you tend to have more bad news for people than good, consider taking a break from reading for others to practice grounding yourself. Your outlook on life or your energies may be affecting your readings. If you feel like you do have a good balance, practice delivering your readings with compassion. Ask if the person is ready to hear something negative, deliver the news, and then be empathetic to let the person know that you are sorry that the reading was not more positive.

If you deliver some bad news to a willing participant, don't dwell on the negative. Move right on to another part of the reading or end the clairvoyant session. It may be tricky, especially if the person is hoping that you will change your mind and paint a picture of a happy ending. It can be an easy and guilty pleasure to spend hours hashing out the gory details, but you should keep your focus on helping the subject of your clairvoyant reading. If there is nothing more to say that will improve the situation, end the session. If the person asks for another session right away, decline for the time being.

Inadvertent scamming

Accepting money for clairvoyant readings can complicate things. Don't get me wrong, I love the business and have done it myself since entering adulthood. However, there are a few social niceties you will have to observe as a clairvoyant business-person. First of all, make sure that psychic reading or fortune-telling is legal where you live. In some localities, all clairvoyant readings for money are assumed to be frauds. If you find yourself bending the definitions of clairvoyant by calling yourself a life coach, spiritual counselor or similar, you may not be acting ethically. Be up front with what it is that you intend to do, and what you cannot do.

You may find it hard to say no to clients when they repeatedly offer you money, but asking like this is inappropriate. The most common of these situations for me involves a client asking for a reading on the same topic over and over again, hoping I will see something different. I've observed that if a client does not change anything in his or her life, the outcome will not change, so I will ask such a client to stop purchasing readings until such time that things have changed significantly.

For example, at the time of this writing, a client has been contacting me about an ex-boyfriend. He is recently divorced and has told her that he does not want a relationship. She has been asking me to see whether he will change his mind and marry her in the future. The future I saw for them was not marriage. In fact, I didn't see marriage in his future at all. When I told the client this, she was justifiably disappointed and asked several clarifying questions, but the answer was still the same. The client asked for another reading on the same man that week, and then again in a month. I asked if she had changed her dealings with him, but they were in the same pattern of an uneasy friendship. I've asked that client not to contact me with readings on him again, since to the best of my ability, my visions have informed me that he is not the one for her if she desires marriage.

Believe me, it breaks my heart to tell a client that I cannot help him or her with goals, but the truth is that I see what I see in my clairvoyant readings, and I cannot twist them. Of course I would love to accept more money to feed my family, but I have to help clients understand how clairvoyance works. The vast majority of those who pay for clairvoyant readings are confident people, and a client usually wants to take control of his or her own destiny. However, for a conspicuous few, it is important to relinquish the control they gift to you.

Negative Emotions

When I perform clairvoyant readings all day, I feel calm but energized, happy, and productive. However, many negative feelings can arise from clairvoyance, especially for those who are untrained in the methods outlined in this book. It is time to go over some of the negative feelings that can manifest when you become a clairvoyant, and how to deal with each of them in a constructive way so that they don't increase and you don't have to give up your clairvoyant practice entirely.

Stress

The main side effect of clairvoyance is stress, especially if you choose to do clairvoyant readings for others and run into some of the problems I've talked about thus far. Performing clair-voyance for yourself can be stressful enough—you can worry about what you see, and you may have difficulty deciding when to do a reading and when to refrain. If you feel stressed out by your clairvoyant practice, take a break from any reading you might be doing for others. Ground yourself so that you don't pick up on others' emotions or do inadvertent clairvoyant readings. When you are pondering whether or not to read for yourself, go back to carefully considering your questions and reframing them if the answer are making you feel trapped. If there is nothing you can change about the situation, do a clairvoyant reading on a different topic instead.

When clairvoyance gets scary

Many who read this book may have decided to do so after a scary clairvoyant experience, such as seeing a ghost or having a vision of a calamity befalling a loved one. Such clairvoyant flashes can be frightening. But hopefully through the use of this book, you've learned to control such visions through grounding, telling entities such as ghosts to go away, and refocusing your mind to only look for constructive visions instead of seeing a sad or scary movie replay itself.

It is important to note that if your clairvoyant visions continue to be scary, stressful, and refuse to be controlled, there may be a deeper problem at hand. Uncontrolled clairvoyant visions may end up being hallucinations. A hallucination is a vision that could be the result of a serious medical problem such as brain tumors, seizure disorders, organ failure, or mental illness. Hallucinations are clear, not just shadowy imaginary glimpses in the corners of your vision, and they occur usually when the person is wide awake. Since both clairvoyant visions and hallucinations are visions, it may seem impossible to tell the difference at times. The best way to find out if you have a problem would be to ask a trusted loved one to help you decide if your visions are becoming a problem for you. Here are some pointers to help you tell the difference between a clairvoyant vision and a hallucination:

1. A hallucination looks no different from anything else in the same room, and you cannot distinguish it from reality. Hallucinations don't reflect what is really happening. They happen without warning and may occur frequently. You cannot control a hallucination to make it go away. Command hallucinations may tell you to do things you don't want to do. Most significantly, hallucinations negatively affect your relationships, work, or ability to take care of yourself.

2. A clairvoyant vision is seen in your mind's eye, or in the same room only under controlled circumstances. Clairvoyant visions tell a spiritual or literal truth. Once you learn the techniques, clairvoyant visions usually only happen when you want them to. A clairvoyant vision will dissipate when you want it to stop, when you ask it to go away, or when you ground yourself. Such visions will empower you with the ability to make choices in your life, and they do not have sustained negative effects on your emotions and everyday life.

3. If you or a caring person in your life believe that you are experiencing hallucinations, *go immediately to an emergency room* to rule out serious medical conditions. If your clairvoyance makes you stressed or frightened in any way such that you suspect they are hallucinations, you owe it to yourself to at least have

the latter ruled out. If you are deemed clear of medical issues, you can dismiss those fears, and that means you can focus more on mastering techniques that can help.

Is being clairvoyant safe?

Some people are frightened of clairvoyant readings, and other people are frightened of being clairvoyant. Your fears are only limited by your imagination. You can worry that you will never return to your body after astral travel, or you can be nervous about seeing an unpleasant future or a ghost. As with just about everything in life, the only thing you really need to fear is the fear which can immobilize you, preventing you from doing what you need to take care of yourself. Remember that clairvoyance is a normal function of your brain and can be experienced by anyone. After all, the images you see exist whether you look at them or not. There is nothing about the process of clairvoyance that can pose a danger to you.

Your attitude, however, can affect the choices you make in your visionary life. If your attitude is fearful, you can make poor choices. If you find that you continue to be fearful of clairvoyance, dial your practice back a bit. You don't have to stop completely or even reduce frequency. Instead, change the nature of your practice to something with which you are more comfortable, such as lucid dreaming or meditation.

As always, bring your common sense with you when you do clairvoyant readings for yourself or others. Sure, you might be seeing wise spirit guides who always tell the truth, or you might simply be getting in touch with the deep honesty of your higher self. But you could also be letting your imagination play tricks on you, or you may be dealing with ghosts or spirits who are tricksters themselves. Clairvoyance can be spiritual without taking everything you see in your visions to be literal truth. Use your analytical brain as soon as you come out of any trance, and you'll soon find that you can mix the eerie power of clairvoyance with the everyday world in a reasonable way.

Bringing Clairvoyance Into the Mainstream

The public perception of clairvoyance isn't all bad. Although there are some who have valid concerns that clairvoyants may be hallucinating or scamming, those rare problems are easy to discover and solve. The vast majority of people you interact with may simply not know what clairvoyance is at all. If you have a vision about somebody and want to ask permission to share it, or if you simply want to tell close family and friends about how valuable clairvoyant practice is to your life, you'll have to start from the ground up. That will mean confronting myths and worries head-on, and moving past them in order to bring new light to clairvoyance.

Social stigma against people who see things

If you lived a few thousand years ago and displayed a talent for clairvoyance, in some locales you would enjoy a lofty status as the community shaman or witch doctor. These days, those who see things that "aren't there" are often ostracized. So you'll have to take care to help people understand that you are not experiencing hallucinations or, worse yet, trying to trick or scam them. Thus, it is important that you don't introduce your clairvoyance by asking someone point blank if you can share a vision with them. Give a little context first about what you're trying to share.

Coming Out as a Clairvoyant

As you build your skills, every little bit of success will make you want to shout it out to the world and involve your clairvoyance in more aspects of your life. That is okay, but you'll have to be just as respectful about your clairvoyant beliefs as you might with religious beliefs that could potentially offend or alienate. It may be best to start out by seeking out other clairvoyants.

Try searching around locally for a psychic fair. Psychic fairs are usually held in a community commons and consist of many different professional psychic readers, including clairvoyants. For your first visit, you don't have to jump in and become a vendor at the fair selling clairvoyant readings, although that is okay too. It might be more inspiring, though, to connect with the other clairvoyants at the fair and share experiences. Collect business cards, make some friends, and bring along enough money to try at least two other clairvoyant readings.

Experiencing someone else's clairvoyant reading can help you grow as a reader. Pay attention to the methods being used, and don't be afraid to ask what is going on. Is the clairvoyant going into a trance or not using a trance state at all? Are any divination tools being used? It can be especially interesting to try a reader who has a new form of divination, but I encourage beginners to experience a clairvoyant reader who uses similar methods to their own with a few more years of practice under his or her belt. Pay special attention to the delivery, too. Recalling small details and use of empathy and compassion make a big difference. And you might just find a mentor you can emulate.

If you have no psychic fairs in your area, you can also find fellowship with other clairvoyants at metaphysical bookstores or perhaps by searching for friends with the same interests online. Otherwise, you might have to be the pioneer in your community to establish these things.

When the time to talk to your friends and family about your clairvoyant experiences comes, it is best to talk to them one on one, instead of springing the news on everyone at the Thanksgiving dinner table. Pick a family member or friend who might be sympathetic to alternative spiritual journeys, and tell him or her you have something very important and special to share about yourself. Hopefully, an announcement warning the person that your revelation is something important to you will cause more careful consideration of what you have to say, and head off any joking.

Be prepared with resources to help explain what clairvoyance is and to allay any concerns your friend or family member might have. This book is good to have with you, especially if you need to flip to definitions of terms you use. It may take them some time to take your clairvoyance as seriously as you do, especially if they've never had any experience with it. For your first discussion, the best you can expect is tolerance, so don't worry if you don't have somebody immediately volunteering for a clairvoyant reading or believing all of what you've said.

You might find that your friends and family are very interested, and want to get involved with clairvoyance themselves. You can start by offering them readings of their own and sharing this book with them, but you might also want to branch out into the community, especially if there are no psychic fairs or other gatherings of clairvoyants in your area. By bringing all of this into the public arena, you can present the clairvoyant as somebody with natural but highly developed skills and abilities. If you're willing, you can even teach a class or hold a clairvoyant book club at a local bookstore or coffee shop. The following can help you to organize discussions and workshops.

Ethical scenarios

It can be a good exercise for beginner clairvoyants to consider ethical quandaries before they are faced with the pressures of reality. For this exercise, really consider each scenario carefully before reading my advice to get a genuine feel for how you would perform if you were put on the spot. All of these scenarios are based on real situations I have encountered with my clients over the years.

....

One night, you have a disturbing lucid dream in which a young man is murdered. The murderer gets away with it in the dream and is on the loose when you wake up. The next day, you see a news story about how a young man has gone missing. The picture they show on television looks exactly like the man in your dream! His parents appear on the screen begging for him to come home or for any kidnappers to release him. His last name is very distinctive, and you are pretty sure that you could easily look up his parents to call them and tell them about your scary dream. What do you do?

Advice: If a murderer is on the loose, you don't want to ignore your clairvoyant vision, as it might hold clues that could prevent any more harm coming to people. However, it is *not* a good idea to contact the parents of the victim directly. If you are wrong, the news could be devastating for no reason, and even if you are right, contacting the victim's family could slow the investigation. Instead, contact the authorities directly though a tip line or non-emergency number. Explain that your vision was a clairvoyant one, so they will be able to set their own priorities for information about the case. After you have ensured the information is in capable hands, your role is over unless you are contacted later on.

....

You decide to offer clairvoyant readings at a two-day charity fundraiser. On the first day, a woman comes for a clairvoyant reading on her love life, and you find out that she is currently seeing two men. By the end of your reading, she announces that she has decided to leave her husband. The next day a man shows up at your booth to buy a clairvoyant reading, and from his name you are pretty sure that he's the husband of the cheating woman you helped the day before. What do you do?

Advice: Client confidentiality is very important, and I personally only breach it in cases of abuse or physical harm. In the above case, I wouldn't tell the man about his wife. And since I would have insider information on the man's wife, I would politely refer that man to another clairvoyant in order to prevent a conflict of interest on my part. In this situation, I am obviously privy to too much information to be able to give an unbiased reading for such a stranger.

....

Your sister wants a clairvoyant reading about her marriage the night before her wedding. You've never really liked her fiancé, and you've already had a vision that told you the marriage would not be successful. She is already nervous and clearly only wants to hear happy news. What do you do?

Advice: This situation is filled with bias. There is no way you can perform this reading and feel good about it. Don't ruin clairvoyant readings for your sister or for yourself by performing this reading. She shouldn't be visiting a clairvoyant at this point anyway, as she has either made up her mind or needs to call off the wedding and see a couples' counselor. Decline to read for her, and wish her the best.

....

A woman approaches you for a clairvoyant reading and nervously tells you that she has been battling cancer and thinks she probably doesn't have long to live. She wants to know exactly when she is going to die so she can make practical decisions about her material belongings and family. She doesn't seem emotional when she tells you this. What do you do?

Advice: Clairvoyant readings can't usually tell somebody exactly when they are going to die because there are so many choices every individual makes in life that affect the outcomes. Gently explain to the woman that finding a death date isn't really the sort of thing you can offer. Help her find another question that might help more, such as what she should be focusing on to feel that her life is complete and all her affairs in order, ensuring she is well prepared for any outcome.

....

A man comes to you for a clairvoyant reading and asks you if you can tell him whether he has AIDS. He has already gotten a blood test, but the results won't come for some time, and he wants a clairvoyant reading to ease his mind in the meantime while he waits for word from his doctor. What do you do?

Advice: Explain that a clairvoyant cannot diagnose or cure any disease, and so there would be no way for you to accurately see a medical condition, because you might be seeing some sort of spiritual analogy instead. If he still wants a reading, offer to help him change his question to how he can reduce his stress while he waits.

....

After a breakup, you miss your ex a lot and wonder if your old flame has moved on without you. You know you have seen your ex around with another partner, and you wonder if they are getting busy with each other in the bedroom. You ponder whether you should attempt to have a clairvoyant vision about your ex's current sex life (or lack thereof). What do you do?

Advice: There's no point to doing psychic espionage on an ex. When doing this sort of reading for yourself, try to look into your own future potential instead. If you don't see your ex in your future, perhaps you can see some clues to help inspire you to find new love.

....

Somebody comes to you for a clairvoyant reading and is relieved and overjoyed when you give a positive reading. She tells you that she went to another clairvoyant reader in town who told her she was cursed and charged her five thousand dollars to remove said curse. It sounds like a scam to you, and you know that the clairvoyant in question is still taking on more clients in your town and is very hostile toward other clairvoyants whom she sees as competition. What do you do?

Advice: First, comfort the client and help her understand that she is *not* cursed. Don't confront the clairvoyant yourself. Instead, encourage the client to go to the police about the curse scam. Clients may also be able to report their bad experience to other resources such as the Better Business Bureau, the Federal Trade Commission, or even the attorney general, if applicable.

....

A friend of a friend is excited to hear that you are a clairvoyant. He says that he regularly sees a clairvoyant for business advice, but now he can't afford to pay for his daily clairvoyant readings because he is broke and has lost his job and his home. He wonders if you will do free daily clairvoyant readings for him to help empower him with advice about getting a job and getting his finances in order.

Advice: A clairvoyant reading for your friend at this point would only serve to distract him from what he should really be doing, which is looking for a job. It doesn't take a clairvoyant to see that he should be putting all his energy into his job search, and a reading won't make the unpleasant parts of looking for work go away. Decline to read for him at this point, and ask if you can help him in more concrete ways, like proofreading his résumé.

....

You start dating a really nice person who is a little scared of your clairvoyant "powers." Your new crush is worried that you will use your abilities to find out deep secrets or to otherwise spy on others' lives. If you two want to continue dating, your new love says, could you give up your clairvoyant practice forever? What do you do?

Advice: Before you make any promises you might not keep, you should help your new squeeze understand that being clairvoyant doesn't mean you're omniscient. Chances are that this person's major concerns are unfounded. If the person is adamant, pass on another date—this person is a more than a bit controlling. After all, it doesn't take clairvoyance to see that such emotionally abusive behavior will only get worse.

....

You see a pretty intriguing clairvoyant vision in which you find a large amount of money on the sidewalk at noon on Valentine's Day. It is an incredibly unlikely scenario, and you have to work at noon that day anyway at your day job. Still, you find yourself wondering if you're

*crazy for wanting to play hooky from work and see if
that vivid picture comes true literally. What do you do?*

Advice: Some solutions that you see to problems will be
impractical for whatever reason. That's a great reason to change
your line of questioning. In this case, your next clairvoyant session should be on how to increase your income without risking
your sense of security. There's usually more than one way to get
the same desired outcome.

Honing Your Skills and Practicing: Performing Clairvoyant Readings for Others

As a fortune-teller, the vast majority of my business readings
for others as well as personal readings for members of my
family do not look like séances. Rather, they are usually one-
on-one clairvoyant sessions with another person. Though the
clients may or may not choose to help interpret the symbols
seen (as is done in a séance), clients usually have no interest
in trying to see the clairvoyant visions themselves during my
clairvoyant readings.

As a result, reading for others can be complex; people are
inherently trusting you to not only see the truth clearly, but
they also want you to communicate what you see with accuracy and compassion. There are a number of special ethical
issues that apply to providing readings for others we have
already explored in depth. For now, however, let's assume that
there are no sticky ethical quandaries and you simply want to
use the clairvoyant skills you've developed as a beginner to
help those who choose not to develop their own, or who can't
trust their own biases.

Preparing somebody else for a reading with you

People make a lot of strange assumptions about clairvoyants, so if you are asked for a clairvoyant reading or if you offer one to someone, it is important to have a little talk first about what to expect. As silly as it might sound, you'll probably need to be up front about the fact that you don't know everything there is to know and that you are as prone to making mistakes as any other human being.

You'll also need to decide what the clairvoyant session will be like, and prepare your subject for that as well. For example, if you prefer to go into a trance and meditate for forty minutes every time you do a clairvoyant reading, talk about that and put forth your own expectations for quiet and undisturbed time so your friend isn't peppering you with questions or wondering whether you're taking a little nap while you're trying to concentrate. If you don't want questions during the reading, you can reserve time at the end of the session for clarification.

Consider also that if you're not ready to have a person present while you do a clairvoyant reading, you can offer to come back later with an answer. Delayed response is completely appropriate if you want to do some lucid dreaming on the topic, for example. You may have to explain what techniques you are using; there's a common misconception that a clairvoyant has to be in the same room with a person to give a reading. I like to tell people that I won't be sucking the information out of their brains, so it is okay for me to be doing the reading in another place or at another time.

Finally, coach your subject about which questions are best to ask for your reading. You can review the types of questions given earlier in this chapter and help the person select a question that will be most helpful. Choosing the right question is important not only for managing expectations, but also for getting the most valuable information out of a reading. If a person thinks you are going to predict somebody's death date or that you'll bring back a scorned ex-girlfriend, you can steer them on the right track before embarrassment or disappointment sets in. Carefully gauge your subject's mood as well. If the questions are heavy, ask if he or she is really ready to hear the answer. In many cases, a person wants a clairvoyant reading for confirmation of their biggest hope, and if you can't give them that, the reading isn't considered useful to them. If you see some "bad" questions pop up, this is a red flag that they may have trouble receiving your answer when it turns out that it's not the one they were seeking.

Communicating a reading clearly and well

Communicating a clairvoyant reading to another person can lead to misunderstandings and confusion, especially for a beginner. People who don't know anything about clairvoyance may assume you receive information in much the same way as reading a newspaper, while the actual experience can range from resembling a foreign movie without subtitles, to assuming the nature of a riddle with highly symbolic imagery.

Decide ahead of time if you want the interpretation of the reading to be collaborative—that is, if you want the other person to give input about what you see. As a beginner, there are pros and cons to doing a collaborative reading. On the plus side, symbols may have more meaning to your subject than to yourself, so you might get to take a back seat and let the other person clarify the interpretation. But since you are new to this, you might be slow to experience the images or have trouble finding words to put to what you see. If that happens, the subject may hijack the conversation, or at the very least their interpretations may interrupt your concentration and flow.

Remember to keep your clairvoyant log handy in order to write down what you see or to sketch the imagery, even if a person is there receiving a reading. What you and the other person remember might differ because the things that seem unimportant to both of you will be easily forgotten, even if they turn out to be very important after all. Also, because your talent is still developing, you might come to a sudden realization later regarding the importance or meaning of a vision and need to contact the subject again. Make sure you get the person's phone number or email address. I can't tell you how many times I've gotten up at night to write down something to tell a person who had a reading earlier that day.

Be honest if what you see is confusing or you don't see anything at all. It is hard to read for others. There's an extra element of performance anxiety (possibly even a little stage fright), and when somebody else counts on what you're saying, it might cause you to draw a blank or to be unable to concentrate properly. Offer to try again some other time if things don't work out, and never be afraid to admit that you are still learning. Everybody has to start somewhere; even doctors have to be good students in medical school before they set foot inside a hospital or clinic. It isn't the end of the world if you give somebody a bad reading, either, as long as you manage expectations ahead of time by letting them know you're a beginner.

Hang in there. I can honestly say that being a clairvoyant reader is the most fulfilling profession. Not only do I get to see amazing things and be the fly-on-the-wall witness to other peoples' secrets—I get thanked for it! My clients are some of the most grateful people I know. Sometimes one of them will come back to see me years after a clairvoyant session, just to let me know that a vision of mine came true. So even if you are a little nervous about doing clairvoyant readings for others, I highly recommend giving it a try, if just as a way to hone your skills.

conclusion

With this book you have started your clairvoyant journey of growth through special, easy-to-perform techniques. You've been given the opportunity to master foundational basics like dream recording, grounding, and meditation. You've also been given the tools to branch out to more complex skills like divination, psychometry, astral and ethereal travel, trance work, and the perception of auras.

Now, the only limit to your clairvoyant practice is whatever you set for yourself. You can continue pushing past your comfort zone to master all the techniques and grow your experience, or you can find a set of skills you are comfortable with and develop an expertise within that specialization. You can choose to keep clairvoyant readings a private spiritual practice, or you can make them your business and livelihood.

As a beginner, clairvoyance may seem like a fun trick, but if it truly works for you, I hope you'll begin to integrate it into your life as a source of spiritual strength. Many people turn to prayer or talk with a loved one when faced with serious decisions. Clairvoyance can be another resource you use during times of need, not just another perception. I hope you will be able to trust your clairvoyant senses, even in times of doubt. After all, seeing is believing!

glossary

apparition: A vision of a ghost seen by a clairvoyant.

astral plane: A mental or spiritual plane of existence, considered to be a parallel dimension for the purposes of clairvoyant exercises.

astral travel: The perceived experience of traveling through space in the astral plane.

clairvoyance: The practice of obtaining true information about the past, present or future in a visual form.

clairvoyant: A person who practices clairvoyance.

divination: A system using tools or symbols that are organized for a person to be able to practice looking for signs about the past, present, or future.

energy: The spiritual life force that permeates the universe which is the proposed mode of action for transporting and generating clairvoyant visions.

etheric travel: The perceived mental experience of traveling even though one's body is not physically traveling. Also called an out-of-body experience.

ghost: The energetic signature that may remain after a person dies.

grounding: Balancing out one's own energy level so that one feels alert but calm.

higher self: A conceptual part of the self that is subconscious, infallible and good, often overridden by conscious desires.

lucid dreaming: Having control over one's dreams and being aware of the dream state while still asleep.

omens: Ordinary observations to which meanings are ascribed so that they become psychic predictions.

out-of-body experience: *See* ethereal travel.

poltergeist: A ghost that may have the ability to move objects in the real world.

precognition: The ability to know events that will happen in the future.

psychic: A person who receives information from a source other than the everyday five senses.

psychometry: Being able to sense an object's history as you hold it.

scrying: A way to be clairvoyant while looking at something that sparks your intuition, like a dancing candle flame or the flecks and sparkles inside a crystal ball.

séance: A group clairvoyant session with the aim of receiving messages from a ghost.

seer: See clairvoyant.

spirit journey: A style of visioning in which a person enters a trance and sees a landscape in the mind's eye through which one travels, often encountering spirit people or creatures along the way.

square breathing: Breathing in for four counts, holding your breath for four counts, breathing out for four counts and then holding again for four counts.

visionary: See clairvoyant.

vivid dreaming: Dreaming highly visual dreams in color.

bibliography

Andrews, Ted. *How to See and Read the Aura.* Woodbury, MN: Llewellyn Worldwide, 2006.

BelindaGrace. *You Are Clairvoyant: Simple Ways to Develop Your Psychic Gifts.* Woodbury, MN: Llewellyn Worldwide, 2011.

Buckland, Raymond. *The Weiser Field Guide to Ghosts: Apparitions, Spirits, Spectral Lights and Other Hauntings of History and Legend.* San Francisco: Red Wheel, 2009.

Dale, Cyndi. *Everyday Clairvoyant: Extraordinary Answers to Finding Love, Destiny, and Balance in Your Life.* Woodbury, MN: Llewellyn Worldwide, 2010.

DesPres, Michelle. *The Clairvoyant Path: Follow Your Inner Wisdom to Healing, Empowerment & Change.* Woodbury, MN: Llewellyn Worldwide, 2012.

McElroy, Mark. *Lucid Dreaming for Beginners: Simple Techniques for Creating Interactive Dreams.* Woodbury, MN: Llewellyn Worldwide, 2010.

Owens, Elizabeth. *Spiritualism & Clairvoyance for Beginners: Simple Techniques to Develop Your Psychic Abilities.* St. Paul, MN: Llewellyn Worldwide, 2005.

Tyson, Donald. *Scrying for Beginners: Use Your Unconscious Mind to See Beyond the Senses.* Woodbury, MN: Llewellyn Worldwide, 2011.

Webster, Richard. *Aura Reading for Beginners: Develop Your Psychic Awareness for Health & Success.* Woodbury, MN: Llewellyn Worldwide, 2008.

———. *The Complete Book of Auras: Learn to See, Read, Strengthen & Heal Auras.* Woodbury, MN: Llewellyn Worldwide, 2011.

To Write to the Author

If you wish to contact the author or would like more information about this book, please write to the author in care of Llewellyn Worldwide, and we will forward your request. Both the author and publisher appreciate hearing from you and learning of your enjoyment of this book and how it has helped you. Llewellyn Worldwide cannot guarantee that every letter written to the author can be answered, but all will be forwarded. Please write to:

Alexandra Chauran
℅ Llewellyn Worldwide
2143 Wooddale Drive
Woodbury, MN 55125-2989

Please enclose a self-addressed stamped envelope for reply, or $1.00 to cover costs. If outside the USA, enclose an international postal reply coupon.

Spiritualism & Clairvoyance for Beginners
Simple Techniques to Develop Your Psychic Abilities
Elizabeth Owens

Margaretta and Catherine Fox's successful communication with a spirit entity in 1848 sparked a new understanding of the spirit world in the United States. This new movement is called Modern Spiritualism. Based on Spiritualism's rich tradition, Elizabeth Owens demonstrates how one can develop natural clairvoyant skills in order to hear the "wisdom of the spirits."

Emphasizing patience and practice, the author insists that clairvoyance is possible for everyone. She explains many forms of clairvoyance (psychometry, clairsentience, clairaudience, and so on), and offers examples based on her own experiences and those of six other spiritualist mediums. Exercises in meditation, memory development, visualization, and symbol interpretation progressively help readers enhance and cultivate their own innate gift of the "sixth sense."

978-0-7387-0707-5, 192 pp., 5 $^3/_{16}$ x 8   **$13.99**

So
You
Want
to Be
a
PSYCHIC
INTUITIVE?

A Down-to-Earth Guide

Alexandra Chauran

So You Want to Be a Psychic Intuitive?
A Down-to-Earth Guide
ALEXANDRA CHAURAN

Dependable guidance, communication with departed loved ones, helping friends and family—the lifelong rewards of a strong psychic connection are countless. Whether you're a beginner or already in touch with your intuition, this encouraging, conversational, and hands-on guide can help you strengthen your psychic skills. Featuring illustrative anecdotes and easy exercises, you'll learn how to achieve a receptive state, identify your source of information, receive messages, and interpret coincidences, dreams, and symbols. Step-by-step instructions make it easy to try a variety of psychic techniques and divination, such as telepathy, channeling, spirit communication, automatic writing, and scrying. There's also practical advice for wisely applying your enhanced psychic skills personally and professionally.

978-0-7387-3065-3, 264 pp., 5 ³/₁₆ x 8   **$14.95**